Current Perspectives:
Readings from InfoTrac® College Edition

Forensics and Criminal Investigation

David Kotajarvi

WADSWORTH
CENGAGE Learning

Australia • Brazil • Japan • Korea • Mexico • Singapore • Spain •
United Kingdom • United States

WADSWORTH
CENGAGE Learning

ISBN-13: 978-0-495-59778-0
ISBN-10: 0-495-59778-3

Wadsworth
10 Davis Drive
Belmont, CA 94002-3098
USA

Cengage Learning is a leading provider of customized learning solutions with office locations around the globe, including Singapore, the United Kingdom, Australia, Mexico, Brazil, and Japan. Locate your local office at:
www.cengage.com/international

Cengage Learning products are represented in Canada by Nelson Education, Ltd.

To learn more about Wadsworth, visit
www.cengage.com/wadsworth

Purchase any of our products at your local college store or at our preferred online store
www.ichapters.com

For product information and technology assistance, contact us at
Cengage Learning Customer & Sales Support, 1-800-354-9706

For permission to use material from this text or product, submit all requests online at
www.cengage.com/permissions
Further permissions questions can be emailed to
permissionrequest@cengage.com

Printed in Canada
1 2 3 4 5 6 7 12 11 10 09 08

Table of Contents

Preface

Modern criminal investigation is a far cry from the old "gum-shoe". Today's crime scene specialists are scientists with a little artistry thrown in for good measure. They are creative in their techniques and "armed" with scientific gadgets and gizmos that are so gee-whiz that they have spawned several very popular television shows.

Statistics will bear out that violent crime is on the rise, offenders are getting younger, and a higher percentage of offenders are incarcerated. Public interest in crime detection, especially the forensic side, is at an all time high.

The articles included in this reader have been selected to highlight the advancements in crime scene forensics. Along with the rapid improvements in information technology and the techniques used to thwart cyber crime, those men and women responding to the scenes of violent crimes or working in the lab are constantly updating their arsenal.

Microscopic examination of evidence is commonplace in today's crime fighting world. The analysis of trace evidence such as fibers, hairs, soil, paint chips, and others are completed with incredible accuracy and a detail never imagined in the past. Skeletal remains, bodilyy fluids including blood, chemicals, and all substances are reduced to their molecular level and analyzed and identified. The analysis of bullets and firearms has also gone high-tech. All these and the many other forensic tools take the guesswork out of suspect identification. In the courtroom, these methods have been generally accepted and are often used to convince judges and juries of guilt.

Of particular note is the wide spread use of DNA technology. Currently there are over three million criminal offenders in the national data bank. Thousands of "hits," both of new cases and of "cold" cases, have occurred due to DNA evidence from a crime scene matching an offender in the data bank. Canada publishes their National DNA Data Bank statistics every two weeks. From their results it is clear that their use of the data bank is highly successful. One statistic illustrates that over five hundred murder suspects have been fingered through the DNA data bank.

A glimpse into the future of forensics is brain fingerprinting. The lie-detector, or polygraph, is placed on a shelf with the typewriter and phonograph through this innovation. The details of a crime, stored in the suspects' brain, can actually be detected through technology. This chapter should be of particular interest to those intrigued by the advances in the detection of deceit.

The goal of this reader is to inform the criminal justice student of the tremendous strides in the field of crime scene forensics. And yes, much of what you see on television is real and in use in the modern police department and crime lab.

David Kotajarvi

Part 1

Facial Reconstruction, Bones, Identification of Human Remains

1

In Bones, He Sees the Clues from Life

Kareem Fahim

The remains, including a skull, neck, shoulders and hips, sat in bags on a metal gurney in the medical examiner's office in Brooklyn. The detectives thought they knew whom the remains belonged to, but that mattered little to Bradley Adams.

As the city's forensic anthropologist, Dr. Adams was trained to report only what the bones told him. "You go in as much in the blind as possible, so your findings aren't tainted," he said.

Some details he spotted immediately. Looking at the size and features of the assembled bones, he realized they were from a grown man. As he moved his eyes elsewhere, he noticed another thing: Someone had sawed the man apart.

He set about cleaning some decomposing flesh off the bones. "For an anthropologist, the tissue kind of gets in the way," he said.

The police relied on Dr. Adams's exam to confirm the man's identification and to provide clues about the weapons that might have been used to cut him apart. In dozens of cases last year, Dr. Adams performed similar services, analyzing fresh corpses, decomposing bodies or just bones. Since most of those cases are still in the court system, there are limits to what he can discuss.

Dr. Adams, 37, started working for the city's medical examiner's office in August 2004, after he moved with his wife and young son from Hawaii to New Jersey. His predecessor, Amy Zelson Mundorff, who was also the city's first forensic anthropologist, was part of the team that identified the victims of the Sept. 11 terror attack. Ms. Mundorff, who was injured herself when the south tower of the World Trade Center collapsed, spent the next months and years analyzing tens of thousands of body parts.

By the time Dr. Adams took over -- he had not even been in the country during the attacks -- DNA experts more than anthropologists were leading the identification effort. At the same time, crime in New York had fallen to record lows. It seemed his tenure might be less eventful than Ms. Mundorff's.

But that was not to be. Even with the low crime rate, detectives have delivered to Dr. Adams a stream of victims, people killed in accidents or those who committed suicide or people who disappeared.

Then there are homicide victims, including a conspicuous batch who were dismembered after they were killed. Dr. Adams's skills have been particularly useful for those cases, said Dr. Charles S. Hirsch, the city's chief medical examiner. "Finding tool marks on dismembered bones is his specialty," he added, referring to the practice of examining chips, cuts and other marks on a bone to divine what kind of weapon was used.

Dr. Adams's book-filled office on East 30th Street is decorated with travel mementos from his journeys for the Army to identify the remains of missing United States soldiers. During an interview, he talked enthusiastically about studying the bones of dead New Yorkers.

They do not all belong to people. The animal remains from Santeria rituals and perfectly natural pet deaths also occupy his time, he said.

But the bones that the detectives found in May, in two bags near Long Island Rail Road tracks in Brooklyn, were human.

Those bones belonged to Robert Heald, a mentally ill man whose brother-in-law tortured him, the authorities say, locking him in a closet for days at a time and pouring boiling water over him. But Dr. Adams focused on the so-called biological profile, in which he gathered information to determine the age, race, sex and stature from the bones.

He had to be careful. Dr. Adams had corrected the mistaken assumptions of investigators before.

When he was a graduate student in Tennessee, Dr. Adams and another student received a call from the police, who had found a skull and bones in the woods. The police told him they were sure it belonged to a woman who had gone missing. They suspected her husband, Dr. Adams recalled.

"We looked down at the skull, and within five seconds told them, 'This is not the woman you're looking for,' " he said. The skull the officers had found, Dr. Adams determined, belonged to a little girl. "Just to see their faces and how the whole operation changed," he said. "Calls went out, the F.B.I. got involved and they started gathering information on missing children from the area." The body turned out to be that of a 7-year-old girl who had been murdered.

Dr. Adams's childhood included summers at his grandfather's funeral home in Salina, Kan., where he strolled through the embalming room and felt almost no fear of the bodies that he saw there, he said. "I had no idea who they were," he said.

At graduate school, he studied with Dr. William Bass, the forensic anthropologist who maintained an acre of wooded land that contains bodies in varying states of decay to be studied. Dr. Adams went on to work for the Army's Central Identification Lab in Hawaii. From there he saw the world, traveling to Indonesia, Vietnam, Nicaragua and other countries to try to find the remains of thousands of missing soldiers United States soldiers.

He traveled to North Korea four times. "Most of the time, they kept us in a base camp out in the woods surrounded by armed guards," he said. "We weren't able to walk through the streets." On one of his trips, he found 12 soldiers in a mass grave along the east side of the Chosin Reservoir.

When Dr. Hirsch, the medical examiner, offered Dr. Adams a job in New York, he said, the decision was relatively easy. Few big cities have forensic anthropologists on staff, and New York's large population meant that he would never want for interesting and important work.

The death of Mr. Heald was such a case. As he looked at the bones, Dr. Adams looked for so-called false start kerfs -- points in the bones where someone started to cut and then stopped, leaving behind the width of the cutting tool as a clue.

Probably a mechanized power saw, he thought.

Prosecutors say that Mr. Heald's sister watched her husband cut him up with that saw and put his body parts into bags. Then she took the bags, they say, with her daughter trailing, and dumped them by the railroad tracks.

2

Recognition by Forensic Facial Approximation

Case Specific Examples and Empirical Tests

C.N. Stephan, M. Henneberg

*The skeletal remains of one individual found near Adelaide in 1994,
although not known at the time, were the first evidence of what was to be a
serial killing reported to have resulted in the highest casualty list to date in
Australia (12 victims). Since the usual methods of identification could not be
used or were unsuccessful on these remains, facial approximations were
produced and advertised over the 4-year period following their discovery, in
an attempt to help to identify them. However, no identification was made. In
1999, the remains were reported to be identified by radiographic
comparison. Approximately 3 months before this identification was made,
another facial approximation was produced by the first author (CNS), but
this face was never advertised in the media. Although rarely reported in the
literature, this paper provides an example where facial approximation
methods were not successful in a forensic scenario. The paper also reports
on empirical tests of the facial approximation created by the first author to
determine if this facial approximation might have been useful had it been
advertised. The results provide further evidence that high resemblance of a
facial approximation to the target individual does not indicate
recognizability, as the facial approximation was poorly recognized even
though it bore good resemblance to the target individual. The usefulness of
facial approximation techniques is discussed within the context of this case
and more broadly. Methods used to assess the accuracy of facial
approximations are also discussed and further evaluated.*

Introduction

On 16 August 1994, skeletal remains were found in a shallow grave at Lower Light, a rural area just north of the city of Adelaide, Australia. Despite an anthropological report made by the second author (MH) that later proved to be highly accurate as to age, sex and stature, no identification was initially made by the investigating authorities. Upon exhaustion of usual identification methods, facial approximation was attempted. A number of facial approximations were constructed, each by different 'experts' and some at different times over the 4 years following the skeletal find (Fig. 1). Despite advertisement of a number of these facial approximations through both television and newspaper media during the 4 years following the discovery of the remains, police reported no matches. Fig. 1 demonstrates the variability in the appearance of the faces that were constructed and also the variation in the dexterity of the practitioners who produced them.

On 11 January 1999, the first author (CNS) was approached to produce a new facial approximation for the remains found at Lower Light. At this stage the practitioner was relatively new to the field having just completed his first research project on the topic, which was published in a 2001 edition of the Journal of Forensic Sciences [1]. The facial approximation was constructed using published methods available at that time, and the completed face (Fig. 2) was taken to the South Australian police for photography, on 23 February 1999. Although photographed, this facial approximation was never advertised. Three months later, on 20 May 1999, police discovered the remains of eight people, in six plastic vats, in a disused bank in Snowtown, North of Adelaide. This lead to the discovery that four other murders were linked to the people found in the barrels: two more bodies that were buried in the backyard of the accussed's former home; a man found hanging from a tree in Kersbrook, Adelaide in 1997; and the skeletal remains found at Lower Light, in 1994 (as described by numerous media reports). In 1999 the positive identification of the Lower Light remains was reportedly made using X-ray comparison.

Despite the use of now outdated facial approximation methods, the resemblance of the facial approximation (constructed by the first author) to the victim has been reported as high by many individuals. This subjectively assessed similarity has frequently promoted the question "would the face have been recognized if advertised?". While it can never be known if advertisement of the facial approximation would have played a role in an earlier establishment of the victim's identity (since casework is influenced by many confounding factors, e.g., broadness and timing of media coverage, who sees the facial approximation advertisement, etc.) empirical testing can establish if the facial approximation is recognizable from a set of other individual's faces at rates above or not different from chance. Here we report the results of such tests conducted on the facial approximation of the Lower Light skull, and discuss these findings in light of the case and general knowledge of facial approximation techniques.

Methods enabling the assessment of the accuracy of facial approximations have been previously commented on in the literature (see [2] for review). Facial approximation accuracy can be defined in two ways. Facial approximations can be accurate in the sense that they display true anatomical similarity to the target individual or they may be accurate if they are easily correctly recognized [2]. This distinction is significant because facial images that bear little anatomical similarity to the target individuals (e.g., low resolution or pixelated images and caricatures) may still be correctly recognized and even with more ease than faces displaying true anatomical similarity [3-5]. Since the success of facial approximations depends more fundamentally upon correct recognition than similar anatomical morphologies accurate facial approximations are better defined as those that are easily correctly recognized than those that are anatomically similar [2]. Thus, accuracy is used here to refer to the "recognizability" of a facial approximation not necessarily to its similarity with a target individual.

Testing of the accuracy (recognizability) of a facial approximation can be seen to be similar to the scenario in eyewitness identification--the assessor or the judge must make a decision about who is the target individual (often a perpetrator for eyewitness identification, but in the case of facial approximation the person is often a murder victim). For eyewitness identification such tests have been conducted, using living individuals, in three ways: (i) show-ups; (ii) simultaneous line-ups; and (iii) sequential line-ups. Similar protocols can be employed when using facial photographs and these are often reported as face arrays or photo spreads. A show-up presents a single suspect to the witness who must then make a decision to identify, or not to identify, this individual [6]. Show-ups are known to be unfair because they suggest who the suspect is, and the witness has only one person to choose from [6-8]. A simultaneous line-up presents the witness with a number of people from which to choose, so that it is not necessarily apparent to the witness who the suspect is [6]. Despite this advantage, simultaneous line-ups have been found to elicit many false identifications [8-12] seemingly because they encourage relative judgements, i.e., witnesses make decisions based on differences and similarities between line-up members rather than making absolute judgements whether or not each individual is or is not the target [7]. This problem can be overcome using sequential line-up presentation methods, which force witnesses to use a more absolute identification protocol [7]. That is, in sequential line-ups a number of faces are presented one at a time to an assessor who must make an immediate decision if each face is, or is not, the target individual; identifying the face means that the rest of the faces in the sequence will not be seen, and not identifying a face means that it cannot be identified at a later stage. Note that when presenting the images to the assessor the presenter holds more images than that that will be shown so the assessor cannot anticipate the end of the sequence. Such methods have been shown to significantly decrease false identifications, while maintaining rates of correct identifications in contrast to simultaneous line-ups [9-13].

With regard to facial approximation tests, resemblance ratings can be seen to be an extreme degree of a show-up. Assessors know that the target individual is present and then go on to make a resemblance rating (either a statement or a quantitative number) which is taken to indicate the "accuracy" of the facial approximation [14-17]. Resemblance ratings can be argued to be flawed for much the same reasons as show-ups in eyewitness identification as described above: (i) people are probably already biased because they know the person they are judging is the target individual; (Ji) people do not have the option of identifying someone else who may in fact be more similar to the facial approximation, and (iii) ratings of similarity may not correspond closely with recognition responses. Indeed, research has shown that resemblance ratings are not good indicators of facial approximation success as determined by recognition responses in simultaneous line-ups [2], probably as result of (ii) and (iii) above.

To date two published studies have used simultaneous photo arrays to assess facial approximations [1,18] and have generally indicated a low recognition frequency of facial approximations above chance rates, but no studies have used sequential tests so far. Furthermore, studies testing facial approximation accuracy using face arrays have not accounted for biases in their line-ups. Bias may exist for two reasons: (i) the images might be biased (e.g., there may be slight variations in resolution or pose that cause assessors to chose one photograph more than other photos; here referred to as type I bias); and (ii) the selected distractor faces might be biased (e.g., if distractors are highly dissimilar to the target individual, the target might be disproportionately selected in comparison to the other faces as plausibility of the foils is extremely low and thus these foils may not be functional; here referred to as type II bias) [6].

In facial approximation research, type I bias should be of concern for the photographs of the target individual may be distinctive because they are often derived from family photo albums (resolution is usually poor when images are enlarged, etc.). Thus, individuals may be able to tell who the target individual is from the face array without having even seen the facial approximation. Bias can be determined by testing recognition responses to a face array without showing a facial approximation and determining if any faces in the set are recognized above any others. Thus, recognition responses made from a facial approximation should be compared, not only to chance levels (when simultaneous face arrays are used), but also to those recognition rates obtained when facial approximations are not shown to assessors.

Although face arrays free from type I and type II biases may be favourable, there may be limits, particularly with regard to type II bias. Facial approximations may not represent target individuals well enough for the target to be discriminated from a set of similar looking faces (controlling for type II bias), especially in sequential face arrays since the facial approximation may not look much like the target individual to begin with. Thus the inclusion of faces physically similar to the target individual may hamper identification tests. If this is the case, criteria for face selection with regard to type II bias may need to be adjusted from that used in other eyewitness identification tests (see [6]). However, this would clearly demonstrate weakness of facial approximation methods since recognition tests would be made less stringent. This aspect should be subject to further research in the future.

The aims of this paper are, firstly, to provide readers with a case example of facial approximation non-success, and secondly, to specifically assess the accuracy of the facial approximation, constructed by the first author, on the Lower Light skeletal remains. The second aim is achieved by contrasting the three methods of facial approximation assessment (resemblance rating; simultaneous face array; and sequential face array), and by examining type I bias (biases not due to physical appearance of individuals) in the face array set used for testing.

2. Materials and methods

2.1. Constructing the facial approximation

The face was constructed by the first author (CNS) using traditional clay three-dimensional combination methods as reported in the literature at the time of manufacture (early 1999; for review see [1]). The face was built in line with the anthropological report prepared by the second author (MH), which stated that the individual was a male between the ages of 17 and 24 years and who was about 1720 mm in height. The skull was complete except for a portion of the posterior braincase that was broken probably as a result of a blow to the head. Muscle insertions and general robustness of the skull indicated fairly well developed musculature. The skull was cast in dental plaster using a split mould technique similar to that reported by Taylor and Angel [19]. Soft tissue depths according to Helmer [20] were positioned on the skull cast and the combination approach was undertaken in the construction of the face. Prosthetic eyes were positioned centrally in the orbits, the cornea projecting to a tangent in line with the mid-supraorbital and mid-infraorbital rims (this guideline has now been demonstrated to be inaccurate [21,22]). Nose width was determined by dividing the maximum width of the nasal aperture by 0.6 [23]. "American" guidelines were followed to establish nose projection using the "three times the nasal spine rule" ([24-27]--although updated methods are now available [28]). Mouth width was determined following the canine width rule [17,24,25], but with liberal subjective adjustment (this guideline is also now known to be inaccurate [29]). Once the muscles had been built, a sheet of clay (~5 mm thick) was placed over the muscles following examples given by Prag and Neave [17]. The clay sheets were then contoured to give the final face. Ear height was a little larger than nose height, in accordance with findings by Farkas et al. [30]. Although never sighted by the practitioner, it was reported that hair found at the crime scene was fairly short and had a wavy or slightly curly appearance; hence a totally subjective estimation of hair and style was added to the facial approximation (Fig. 2). Since hair cannot be determined from the skull and because the hair reportedly collected was never presented to the first author, it is not surprising that both the hair texture and style are inaccurate on the facial approximation in comparison to the target individual.

2.2. Testing the accuracy of the facial approximation

First the resemblance of the facial approximation to the target individual was established, for this is the approach traditionally taken by other practitioners in the past [14-17]. Since we wanted to make recognition as easy as possible in our other tests, we tested two photographs of the completed facial approximation, one with hair and eyebrows, and one without, to determine which appeared more similar to the target individual. Fifteen adult assessors (six males, nine females: mean age 31 years, standard deviation 10 years) judged the resemblance of both facial approximations to the target individual, giving a score from 0 to 10, and then we selected the face with the highest resemblance for use in our recognition studies.

For the recognition tests a face array was constructed from newspaper images since we had access to the antemortem image of the target individual from a newspaper (Sunday Mail, 6 June 1999). Nine other distractor faces of the same sex, approximate age and approximate pose as the target individual were selected from Australian newspapers and included in the face array. All images were resampled down (pixels removed), scaled and cropped in Adobe[R] Photoshop[R] 6.0 to give images as closely comparable as possible to each other (Fig. 3). No effort was made to select individuals of similar physical appearance (in this case facial appearance) to the target as recommended in usual eyewitness tests. Thus, this face array consisted of a fairly random sample and is expected to provide a scenario favourable for correct recognitions of the facial approximation (the face array may be biased and hence some distractor faces may not be seen to be plausible alternatives to the target individual and/or the facial approximation).

To determine if any type I bias was present in the face array, sequential and simultaneous presentation trials were conducted without the facial approximation. Fifteen adult assessors (11 females, 4 males: mean age 23 years, standard deviation 12 years) who did not recognize, either personally or as having been seen in the media, any of the faces in the face array were asked to determine, without the facial approximation, who the murder victim (target individual) was in the face array. Assessors had no information apart from the photographs themselves to base this decision on. Assessors first participated in the sequential face array presentation and then the simultaneous line-up. In the sequential face array assessors where shown one face image at a time in a random order. Assessors were forced to decide for each face "yes" or "no" if the face was that of the murder victim. Assessors were aware that if they made an identification of "yes" the trial was completed (they would not see the other faces in the sequence during this test) and if they answered "no" that they would not be able to change their mind to this face at a later point in the trial. The investigator (CNS) held more cards than those included in the face array test so that assessors could not anticipate the end of the sequence. In the sequential trial cards were held about 1 m in front of the assessor and at arm's length from the investigator at 90% to his line of sight so investigator cues, if there were any, were not obvious to assessors (who were hopefully concentrating on the cards and hence not attending to any cues, particularly facial ones, if expressed by the investigator). After assessors had made an identification, or if they proceeded through all the faces in the sequence without making an identification, all the faces in the array were presented simultaneously, but in a random order, to the assessor for him/her to change their identification decision from the sequential trial if they so wished.

Twenty new assessors (14 females, 6 males: mean age 20 years, standard deviation 4 years) who did not recognize, either personally or as having been seen in the media, any of the faces in the face array, were recruited for the main project: to attempt to correctly identify who the target individual was from the facial approximation. Identical procedures were followed as indicated above for face pool testing without the facial approximation, except of course that this time the assessors had access to a facial approximation.

Although assessors had the option of not choosing any face in the simultaneous line-up, a chance rate of 10% was used as it was found that almost all assessors selected a face (see Section 3), and hence appeared biased in this respect (according to chance one would expect a 50% response of "not there", instead it seemed all assessors were choosing a face and hence each face in the array had a 10% chance of being selected). Responses were recorded categorically as correct (target face identification) or incorrect (distractor identification or "no identification" response) for statistical analysis. Observed data were compared to expected frequencies by Fisher's Exact tests in the JMP[R] 4.0 statistical package. As we were only interested in responses larger than chance (and because chance rates were so small that lesser differences would be difficult to detect) confidence intervals for one tailed tests were used.

3. Results

Assessor's resemblance ratings of both facial approximations were in accordance with previous indications from other individuals, including other forensic facial approximation experts, that resemblance was high. It is worth noting that Betty Pat Gatliff, a high profile forensic artist and facial approximation practitioner, indicated to the first author in 2000 that the face appeared similar enough that she would have expected a positive result had it been advertised. Both facial approximations received high, but similar, resemblance rating results (around 7 out of 10), although the facial approximation without hair tended to be rated higher than the facial approximation with hair (Fig. 4). Data distributions for the no hair facial approximation displayed slightly more left skew than those for the facial approximation with hair (Fig. 4). Hence in recognition tests reported here we used the facial approximation without hair as this is expected to favour positive recognition responses according to traditional facial approximation theory (greater resemblance, greater accuracy and possibly more frequent correct recognitions).

Sequential and simultaneous face array tests, done without assessors seeing a facial approximation, showed that the target individual (face number 4) was identified at rates well above other individuals (Fig. 5) and that responses were highly similar between the sequential and simultaneous presentation methods. For sequential line-ups, the identification of the target individual (face number 4) in comparison to other faces was statistically significant ($p < 0.08$) in six out of nine cases (i.e., for face numbers 1, 2, 5, 6, 7, and 8), although the other three cases (face numbers 3, 9, and 10) followed similar trends. In no case was a "not there" response made for either the sequential or the simultaneous face array. During post-experiment feed back assessors expressed their thoughts why they thought they could tell who the murder victim was without the facial approximation. Frequently these explanations included: "the target photograph ... would not be flattering", "... would not be clear", and/or "... would present the person smiling".

When the facial approximation without hair was presented to assessors who then attempted to identify the target individual from the sequential face array, identification of the target individual (face number 4) did not increase (Fig. 6). Face number 4 was not identified above chance rates at statistically significant levels. Face number 4 was also identified somewhat less, but not at rates statistically different from that observed when the facial approximation was not presented to assessors (in both sequential and simultaneous procedures). During sequential trials the majority of responses were the default response of "no identification", as most individuals (60%) completed the sequential presentation without identifying any face. The increased number of "not there" responses for the sequential face array, facial approximation present scenario, was highly statistically significant ($p < 0.001$) in comparison to: (i) the sequential face array, facial approximation not present scenario; (ii) the simultaneous face array, facial approximation not present scenario; and (iii) the simultaneous face array, facial approximation present scenario. Thus, when facial approximations were presented to assessors in the facial approximation present scenario, the number of false identifications decreased in comparison to all other testing conditions.

4. Discussion

The similarity ratings of the facial approximation to the target individual clearly indicate high resemblance, as the modes observed for the facial approximations were high (7 out of 10 for the facial approximation with hair; and 6/10 and 8/10 for facial approximations without hair; Fig. 4). Such resemblance ratings seem comparable with reports of resemblance ratings for other "successful" facial approximations [14-17]. However, despite attempts to encourage "favourable" recognition results here (by using the facial approximation that achieved the highest resemblance, and not selecting a face pool that included distractors who looked like the target individual) recognition frequencies of the target individual were poor, and in fact tended to be less than those when assessors made an identification without the use of the facial approximation. Furthermore, when assessors used the facial approximation in sequential trials the "no identification responses" increased dramatically in contrast to responses when facial approximations were not used. These results offer strong support for claims that resemblance ratings do not indicate the recognizability, and hence accuracy, of facial approximations [2], and that facial approximations are not recognized frequently or reliably above rates expected by chance [1].

Results were also consistent with eyewitness research that indicates sequential face arrays are preferable to simultaneous presentations [9-13]. Sequential face arrays were found to dramatically reduce the number of false identifications whilst not greatly affecting the rate of correct identifications [9-13]. This suggests that the high numbers of false hits in other studies (see e.g. [1]) using simultaneous testing procedures may be a result of the protocols employed not due to recognitions of the facial approximations alone. Therefore, the primary weakness of the facial approximation method seems to be a lack of frequent correct recognitions, rather than a vast number of false recognitions. These findings suggest that sequential face array procedures should be employed in future facial approximation research.

The lack of identification of distractor face numbers 5, 8 and 10 in recognition tests that included the facial approximation indicates that these distractor faces were not functional. That is, these faces were so dissimilar to the facial approximation that they were essentially ignored by assessors. This could be interpreted as meaning that facial approximation methods used here successfully eliminated 30% of the sample, which may perhaps be useful in forensic casework. However, we suspect that such elimination of people to whom the skull does not belong does not require the specific construction of a facial approximation, but rather it can be achieved by the use of a general description of the person's physical characteristics as evident from the skull (e.g., broadness of face, etc.). Consequently, the lack of the identification of face numbers 5, 8, and 10 is probably better interpreted as resulting from type II bias in the face array. After all, the logic for constructing the facial approximation in the first instance is that the visual representation of the face should enable finer discrimination between individuals in contrast to a general written or verbal description. This bias in the face array acts to increase the chance level of correct identifications from 10% to 14%, suggesting that the success of the facial approximation method as observed with 10 faces is actually much less (and should only be considered with respect to 7 faces in the array).

Although the large number of correct identifications made by assessors without ever seeing the facial approximation may be surprising, this can be rationally explained. As indicated in Section 1, many antemortem images obtained of target individuals are of poor resolution as these images have often been enlarged from amateur photographs. The general quality and resolution of the image of the target individual used in this study was rather poor, and this was the reason why other distractor images were resampled down. Despite these attempts it was difficult to get the pictures exactly the same even though all images were printed in newspapers. This can be attributed to the professional shooting of distractor faces (appropriate zoom, lighting, etc.) in contrast to the probable amateur shooting of the target individual under less optimal conditions. Although face numbers 2 and 10 were successfully made to be of poor quality, the target face image (face number 4) still stands out as being different (Fig. 4). We suspect this, combined with each assessor's preconceptions of how a murder victim can be identified from a photograph, enabled a number of assessors to correctly determine who the target individual actually was. Assessor familiarity with the case or individuals in the face array can be discounted as a possible factor because assessors were requested to indicate if they recognized any of the faces either personally or as being seen in the media during the experimental trials. Two individuals tested for the face array facial approximation not present scenario, and one individual in the face array facial approximation present scenario reported familiarity with one or more individuals in the face array and were excluded from analyses reported here. These findings stress the need for any face array used for facial approximation testing to be subjected to tests for type I bias as slight variations in image capture of target individuals in contrast to the distractor faces (including orientation, lighting, pose, expression, etc.) may invalidate facial approximation tests.

Although this study adds further support to findings that resemblance ratings do not indicate the recognizability, and hence accuracy, of facial approximations [2] and that facial approximations are rarely recognized above chance rates [1], these findings do not indicate, that "facial approximation would be detrimental to any forensic identification case" ([22], p. 12, [31], p. 112), or that facial approximations will never yield successful recognitions in any instance. These points need to be highlighted because they have been confused in the literature on a number of previous occasions. Identifications made from facial approximations in some instances by single individuals may result from specific and purposeful recognition by an individual, even if the overall summative rates of recognition in identification tests across individuals are not above chance levels. However, the low frequency of correct identifications suggests that the ability of facial approximations to provoke reliable recognition responses is not strong. If the facial approximation studied here generated correct recognition responses similar to that observed in other identification scenarios when the same individual's face is used, then correct recognitions should have accounted for close to 70% of all recognitions (see e.g. [32]). Recognition responses approximating this value, or even about 50% for example, should have been easily observable within our sample if they actually existed--but they did not.

The findings in this study that the recognition rate of the target individual was less than 50% and not different from chance rates at statistically significant levels, do not indicate that these recognition rates do not absolutely differ from chance rates. With very large samples recognition rates that differ very little from chance may be found to be statistically significant, however, the value of such small rates must be rationally evaluated. If facial approximations do not produce recognition rates above 50%, little confidence can be placed in identifications made by single random individuals. In forensic cases such scenarios are frequent, often with just one or a few individuals coming forward with identification statements, so if facial approximation methods are to offer some degree of reliability they must generate correct recognition responses more than 50% of the time. Until then, facial approximation methods can only be regarded as being unreliable and inaccurate. Also, while correct recognition rates of facial approximations are found to infrequently differ from chance rates, facial approximations cannot be said to provoke purposeful and specific recognitions. Of course, successful recognitions may be more frequent if other information is advertised along with the facial approximation in forensic cases, but then success is not solely dependent upon, and may have little to do with, recognition of the face that has been built on the skull [1,2, 33-35].

Whilst current facial approximation methods are widely recognized as "last resort techniques", the abilities of the methods often appear to be much overstated [35-38]. This may contribute to decreased facial approximation success because judges have no realistic idea of what criteria they should be basing their decisions on. It may be that people familiar with facial approximation techniques (i.e., who know their strengths and weaknesses) can identify the constructed faces more accurately than lay individuals for they know what to look for and what to use in their identification decisions. For example, if it is known that the shape of the vermillion borders of the lips or the shape of the nose cannot be predicted well, but that the general position of features such as mouth location over teeth and ratio of face height to width can be well predicted, then it would seem rational not to use shape of vermillion borders or nose, but to use location of mouth and ratio of face height to width. But people will only know which features to use and which to ignore, if they are made aware of what the methods can realistically achieve. This aspect demands further attention because if it occurs, accuracy rates could be increased by openly educating the public about what facial approximation methods can or cannot realistically do, rather than overstating the accuracy and abilities of the methods as often seems to have been done in the past.

It can never be known if the facial approximation constructed by the first author would have been recognized if it had been advertised in the media before the identification had been made using other methods. Despite apparent similarity of the facial approximation to the target individual, tests here indicate that recognition frequencies of this facial approximation were low (and possibly even hampered by the facial approximation in contrast to identification tests without the use of the facial approximation). However, it only takes one individual to think they recognize the face (for whatever reason, and perhaps not as a result of specific and purposeful facial identification) for the facial approximation to be a success. Consequently it is possible that the facial approximation may have worked but it seems the likelihood for specific and purposeful facial recognition would have been low.

5. Conclusions

The Lower Light case presents a further example where advertised facial approximations have proved unsuccessful. The only other examples of facial approximation non-success reported in the literature appear to be by Haglund and Reay [34], however we suspect it is much more frequent than that reflected by the literature published to date. Furthermore, empirical tests of the facial approximation studied here illustrate that: (i) high resemblance does not necessitate recognition; (ii) correct recognitions of the facial approximation were infrequent; (iii) sequential face array methods are better in comparison to other assessment methods and should be used for determining facial approximation accuracy in the future; and (iv) for the case presented here, advertisement of the facial approximation constructed by the first author soon after its construction may have resulted in a successful recognition but probably as a result of chance, not specific face recognition.

Acknowledgements

Thanks go to Dr. M. Ricci and Dr. E. Pierce for assisting with participant recruitment for the study.

References

[1] C. Stephan, M. Henneberg, Building faces from dry skulls: are they recognized above chance rates? J. Forensic Sci. 46 (2001) 432-440.

[2] C. Stephan, Do resemblance ratings measure the accuracy of facial approximations, J. Forensic Sci. 47 (2002) 239-243.

[3] V. Bruce, A. Young, In the Eye of the Beholder, Oxford University Press, New York, 1998.

[4] G. Rhodes, S. Brennan, S. Carey, Identification and ratings of caricatures: implications for mental representations of faces, Cognitive Psychol. 19 (1987) 473-497.

[5] P.J. Benson, D.I. Perrett, Perception and recognition of photographic quality facial caricatures: implications for the recognition of natural images, Eur. J. Cognitive Psychol. 3 (1991) 105-135.

[6] R.S. Malpass, P.G. Devine, Measuring the fairness of eyewitness identification lineups, in: S.M.A. Lloyd-Bostock, B.R. Clifford (Eds.), Evaluating Witness Evidence: Recent Psychological Research and New Perspectives, John Wiley and Sons, New York, 1983, pp. 81-102.

[7] G.L. Wells, What do we know about eyewitness identification? Am. Psychol. 48 (1993) 553-571.

[8] R. Gonzalez, P.C. Ellsworth, M. Pembroke, Response biases in lineups and showups, J. Pers. Soc. Psychol. 64 (1993) 525-537.

[9] R.C.L. Lindsay, J.A. Lea, G.J. Nosworthy, J.A. Fulford, J. Hector, V. LeVan, C. Seabrook, Biased lineups: sequential presentation reduces the problem, J. Appl. Psychol. 76 (1991) 796-802.

[10] R.C.L. Lindsay, G.L. Wells, Improving eyewitness identifications from lineups: simultaneous versus sequential lineup presentation, J. Appl. Psychol. 70 (1985) 556-564.

[11] R.D. Melara, T.S. DeWitt-Rickards, T.P. O'Brien, Enhancing lineup identification accuracy: two codes are better than one, J. Appl. Psychol. 74 (1989) 706-713.

[12] R.C.L. Lindsay, J.A. Lea, J.A. Fulford, Sequential lineup presentation: technique matters, J. Appl. Psychol. 76 (1991) 741-745.

[13] B.L. Cutler, S.D. Penrod, Improving the reliability of eyewitness identification: lineup construction and presentation, J. Appl. Psychol. 73 (1988) 281-290.

[14] W.M. Krogman, The reconstruction of the living head from the skull, FBI Law Enforcement Bull. 17 (1946) 11-17.

[15] T. Suzuki, Reconstitution of a skull, Int. Crim. Police Rev. 264 (1973) 76-80.

[16] R.P. Helmer, S. Rohricht, D. Petersen, F. Mohr, Assessment of the reliability of facial reconstruction, in: M.Y. Iscan, R.P. Helmer (Eds.), Forensic Analysis of the Skull, Wiley/Liss, New York, 1993, pp. 229-246.

[17] J. Prag, R. Neave, Making Faces: Using Forensic and Archaeological Evidence British, Museum Press, London, 1997.

[18] C.C. Snow, B.P. Gatliff, K.R. McWilliams, Reconstruction of facial features from the skull: an evaluation of its usefulness in forensic anthropology, Am. J. Phys. Anthropol. 33 (1970) 221-228.

[19] R.G. Taylor, C. Angel, Facial reconstruction and approximation, in: J.G. Clement, D.L. Ranson (Eds.), Craniofacial Identification in Forensic Medicine, Oxford University Press, New York, 1998, pp. 177-185.

[20] R. Helmer, Schadelidentifizierung durch elekronicshe bildmischung: sugl el beitr zur konstitutionsbiometrie U Dickermessung d Gesichtsweichteile, Krminalistik-Verlag, Heidelberg, 1984.

[21] C.N. Stephan, Facial Approximation: falsification of globe projection guideline by exophthalmometry literature, J. Forensic Sci. 47 (2002) 1-6.

[22] C.M. Wilkinson, S.A. Mautner, Measurement of eyeball protrusion and its application in facial reconstruction, J. Forensic Sci. 48 (2003) 12-16 (technical note).

[23] B.E. Hoffman, D.A. McConathy, M. Coward, L. Saddler, Relationship between the piriform aperture and interalar nasal widths in adult males, J. Forensic Sci. 36 (1991) 1152-1161.

[24] B.P. Gatliff, Facial sculpture on the skull for identification, Am. J. Forensic Med. Pathol. 5 (1984) 327-332.

[25] W.M. Krogman, The Human Skeleton in Forensic Medicine, Charles C Thomas, Illinois, 1962.

[26] B.P. Gatliff, K.T. Taylor, Three-dimensional facial reconstruction on the skull, in: K.T. Taylor (Ed.), Forensic Art and Illustration, CRC Press, Boca Raton, 2001, pp. 419-475.

[27] K.T. Taylor, Two-dimensional facial reconstruction from the skull, in: K.T. Taylor (Ed.), Forensic Art and Illustration, CRC Press, Boca Raton, 2001, pp. 361-417.

[28] C.N. Stephan, M. Henneberg, W. Sampson, Predicting nose projection and pronasale position in facial approximation: a test of published methods and proposal of new guidelines, Am. J. Phys. Anthropol. 122 (2003) 240-250.

[29] C.N. Stephan, Facial approximation: an evaluation of mouth width determination, Am. J. Phys. Anthropol. 121 (2003) 4857.

[30] L.G. Farkas, I.R. Munro, J.C. Kolar, The validity of neoclassical facial proportion canons, in: L.G. Farkas, I.R. Munro (Eds.), Anthropometric Facial Proportions in Medicine, Charles C Thomas, Illinois, 1987, pp. 57-56.

[31] C.M. Wilkinson, R.A.H. Neave, D. Smith, How important to facial reconstruction are the correct ethnic group tissue depths? in: M. Colonna, M. Belviso, A. Addante (Eds.), Proceedings of the 10th Biennial Scientific Meeting of the International Association for Craniofacial Identification, Bari, 2002, pp. 111-121.

[32] P.J.B. Hancock, V. Bruce, A.M. Burton, Recognition of unfamiliar faces, Trends Cognitive Sci. 4 (2000) 330-337.

[33] W.D. Haglund, Forensic "art" in human identification, in: J.G. Clement, D.L. Ranson (Eds.), Craniofacial Identification in Forensic Medicine, Arnold, London, 1998, pp. 235-243.

[34] W.D. Haglund, D.T. Reay, Use of facial approximation techniques in identification of Green River serial murder victims, Am. J. Forensic Med. Pathol. 12 (1991) 132-142.

[35] C.N. Stephan, Anthropological facial "reconstruction"-recognizing the fallacies, "unembracing" the error, and realizing method limits, Sci. Justice 43 (2003) 193-199.

[36] V. Suk, Fallacies of anthropological identifications, Publications de la Facultae des sciences de l'Universitae Masaryk, vol. 207, 1935, pp. 3-18.

[37] M.F.A. Montagu, A study of man embracing error, Technol. Rev. 49 (1947) 345-347.

[38] G.J.R. Maat, Facial reconstruction: a review and comment, Talanta 30/31 (1998-1999) 247-253.

3

'Let the Bones Talk' is the Watchword for Scientist-Sleuths

Forensic Anthropology at the Smithsonian Institution

Elizabeth Royte

Forensic anthropologists Douglas Ubelaker and Douglas Owsley work at the Smithsonian involves solving mysteries by piecing together unearthed bones. Their work involves mostly historical research such as cause of demise of tribes or native races; but they also work on crime-related matters.

It is late on a Thursday afternoon before Douglas Owsley can turn his attention to the cardboard box on his office floor. He shoves it toward a table and casually lifts the lid. He reaches into wrinkled white sheets and a blanket and pulls out a waxy brown skull.

Bone by bone, Owsley transfers the skeleton to his examination table. "Heavy brow, large mastoid processes, well-defined nuchal [nape of the neck] area," he murmurs, turning the skull this way and that. "Narrow nasal width, pronounced nasal spine. Definitely white, definitely male." But it doesn't take a physical anthropologist to deduce this much information. A medical examiner had supplied the man's identity. What the local pathologist wants Owsley to determine is whether this man, who had disappeared from a nursing home, had suffered any kind of trauma. The bones had been found in a wooded area near the home. It appeared that the gentleman had simply wandered off. Or had he?

Douglas Owsley works as a forensic anthropologist at the Smithsonian's National Museum of Natural History. Strong, compact and encircled by a tooled Western belt, he's the kind of person who doesn't hesitate to get down onto his bare office floor, if that's where the next box of bones lies. His scholarly work involves prehistoric and pioneer bones in the Great Plains and more recent bones in the East. But he also does forensic work. Police departments and medical examiners across the country routinely enlist Owsley's services. They come upon bones and want to know: Who is it? What happened? A forensic pathologist--in the mode of television's Quincy--asks similar questions, but Owsley's work picks up where Quincy's leaves off.

Most of his cases originate in rural areas, because bodies that come to rest in cities are usually found before soft tissues rot away. Dogs discover a fair number of bodies. So do hunters, in the woods after the leaves have dropped, and drivers, in any season, who stop to relieve themselves in wooded sites along roadways.

Owsley works in a cluttered suite of offices on the third floor of the museum. Scientific journals line his shelves, photographs of his buddies exhuming graves hang on the walls. Outside his door, the corridors are institutionally lighted and lined with drawer after wooden drawer, stacked 14 feet high. Here the skeletons of 30,000 people are carefully arranged and catalogued. The bones--of people ranging in age from prenatal to 90, who died between 10,000 years ago and one--hail from as far as Ecuador and Iraq, and as near as Bethesda, Maryland.

A forensic investigation usually begins with the opening of a package. Sometimes Owsley can resolve a case without even sitting down.

Police officer: Is this bone human?

Owsley: No, it's pig.

Officer: Thank you, goodbye.

More often, the inquiry will take weeks or months to play out. Owsley recently finished the case of a Baltimore police officer who denied any involvement in the slaying of his girlfriend. But investigators vacuumed up tiny bone chips--about the size of pencil points--from the back floor of his pickup. Owsley examined the chips under a stereozoom microscope and determined they belonged to somebody whose skull became fragmented perimortem--at or around the time of death. He found traces of soot, lead and blood on the fragments, features consistent, as they say, with those of a bullet fired at close range. "But it's the tiny traces of blood on the bone chips that helped nail him," Owsley says. "It shows up as red rust stains under the microscope." The officer was eventually sentenced to life plus 20 years.

Meanwhile, Nursing Home Man lies on the table, his hand bones in one pile, his foot bones in another. Owsley sorts through the ribs, arranging 12 on the right and 11 on the left. "Hmmm," he says, not overly concerned. Then he picks up a short bone--"rabbit," he says--and sets it aside. It's not unusual to find animal bones with human: the dog that finds bones and buries them under the back porch is not discriminating.

Owsley starts to calculate the man's height, based on the length of his leg and arm bones. He looks at the points where muscles were attached to bone, to get an idea of his build. A creative forensic anthropologist may look at, for example, the ridges where muscles attach on finger bones and wonder if this unidentified skeleton once played the flute, but he'd never include such speculation in a final report. "The science on that is a little flaky," says Douglas Ubelaker, who, as the other forensic anthropologist at the museum, works about 40 law-enforcement cases a year. (He also teaches at George Washington University.) "It could lead investigators to look for missing flute players and rule out all others."

Ubelaker and Owsley are both infuriatingly cautious. "Let the bones talk to you" is their motto. Scientists to the core, they make conclusions based solely on the evidence at hand. "You can't go on your gut feelings," says Ubelaker, sober, mustachioed and, on a summer day when the air conditioning is not working, dressed in sandals, a blue polo shirt and pleated slacks. "A prosecutor comes in, he's convinced it's this guy, and he says, 'Doc, what do you think?' There's a subtle pressure to support his opinion. But you must divorce yourself from that. I'm not an advocate for the FBI or the defense but a spokesman for the victim." I ask if he's ever been wrong. "I don't recall ever being very wrong in a forensic case, considering the evidence available at the time." Though he sounds smug, he is not. He is stating a fact. "You shouldn't be wrong on a report. I won't say it's the skeleton of a person 37 years old, but I will say with 90 percent certainty he's between 30 and 38."

Sixty years ago, the use of anthropology to solve crimes was virtually unheard of. The law-enforcement community didn't recognize that skeletons contained clues that were inaccessible through conventional forensic examinations, and anthropologists, for their part, were reluctant to get involved in police work. Applied science--using anthropology to achieve an immediately tangible result--was somehow less pure than basic research, went the thinking.

Today, forensic anthropology is an accepted science. The American Board of Forensic Anthropology certifies new diplomates each year (Ubelaker is the current president). At the Smithsonian, forensic anthropology began in the 1930s when the Federal Bureau of Investigation moved in across the street on Constitution Avenue.

Ales Hrdlicka, director of the Division of Physical Anthropology from 1903 until 1943, formalized the relationship, and in 1942 Hrdlicka's student and successor, T. Dale Stewart, began to consult regularly for the FBI. In the 1950s Stewart helped in the identification of Korean War dead. But it was the bow-tied, cigar smoking Larry Angel (Smithsonian, February 1977), who worked so many cases in the 1970s that the press started calling him "Sherlock Bones."

(Other Smithsonian scientists also are taking on forensic missions. Roxie Laybourne, an ornithologist [March 1982], has taught several graduate students about identifying feathers found at plane crashes and murder scenes. And there are practitioners of forensic geology and entomology. Geologists can often tell from dirt particles in a victim's clothing where a murder actually happened. Entomologists can tell by what insects are present on a body how long the person has been dead.)

Even now it's not all smooth sailing within the scientific community. "Some anthropologists still think it's technical, not research oriented," says Owsley, heatedly, "but it is research oriented! The information we derive immeasurably improves our work on older skeletons. We look at Civil War digs, at whites versus blacks, old versus young, urban versus rural, rich versus poor, and we see changes in health trends. We can follow health trends through time. We see the results not only of bone cancer, but breast cancer, which metastisizes and perforates bone. We can now track the evolution of warfare among Plains Indians for 6,000 years by bone pathology."

Owsley and Ubelaker enjoy their law-enforcement cases but they both favor historical work--Owsley studying the bones of Colonial villagers and Native Americans, Ubelaker working in Ecuador and in museum collections in Europe, tracing the history of diseases. In studying ancient bones, physical anthropologists are less interested in individuals--how a man fractured his pelvis and why he was buried with his dog--than in documenting what happened to communities over time and space: what they ate, how and where they lived, what diseases afflicted them, how their life expectancy changed as they abandoned the nomadic life for agriculture.

Says Owsley, "We apply what we learn from archaeological excavations to criminal cases, and vice versa. The information flows both ways." Owsley's work with the victims of a prehistoric war who had been dismembered immediately after death proved to be invaluable experience when he worked on the case involving Jeffrey Dahmer's first victim. He analyzed hundreds of bone and tooth fragments that Dahmer had crushed with a heavy implement and scattered over a two-acre site, examined each for cut marks and determined the age and sex of the victim. The Smithsonian's Ralph Chapman clinched the identification by digitizing bitewing x-rays taken by a dentist so they could be scaled to match images from the remains. A second molar root was identical to a 90 percent probability.

Douglas Owsley grew up in a small Wyoming town, the son of a fish and game warden. He entered the University of Wyoming as a zoology major, planning on a career in medicine, or perhaps dentistry. That changed when he volunteered one summer to help George Gill, a charismatic anthropology professor, work a thousand-year-old burial site in Mexico. They mucked around mangrove swamps all day and ate huge shrimp cocktails at night. "I said to myself, `This is the life,'" recalls Owsley, grinning. "I got completely caught up in it." He switched his major, earned his doctorate in physical anthropology under Gill at the University of Tennessee, then began teaching at Louisiana State University in 1980. The crime rate around Baton Rouge and the preponderance of bayous for dumping bodies meant plenty of hands-on forensic cases. In 1987 the Smithsonian sent out a call for a new physical anthropologist and Owsley applied. Today, Gill and Owsley continue their work together, most recently in the analysis of late prehistoric and historic period skeletons from Easter Island.

Douglas Ubelaker also slipped into anthropology after accepting, as a lark, a summer job on a dig. He was a premed student at the University of Kansas when an anthropology professor noted his muscles and invited him on a dig in the Dakotas. The keen-eyed professor was William Bass of the University of Tennessee, who has trained the majority of the forensic anthropologists in the country. To Ubelaker, the prospect of studying centuries-old remains held a "distinct element of romance." He, too, was instantly hooked, and by the end of the summer the Ubelakers knew there would not be another doctor in the family.

Drafted in 1968, just after graduating from college, Ubelaker was assigned to a military hospital lab in Washington, D.C. He spent his spare time working in the Smithsonian's collections, incidentally forging the alliances that would secure him a job at the museum after he earned his doctorate in Kansas.

Both Ubelaker and Owsley appreciate the mystery in their law-enforcement cases, but they try not to get too involved: the bones come and go, and often they don't find out what becomes of a case once their role--pinpointing the age of a bone's owner or suggesting a probable murder weapon--is finished. Knowing a victim's vocation and personal habits could prejudice their investigations. Working on decomposing bodies at the Branch Davidian compound in Waco, Texas, Ubelaker didn't want to know which cult members were still unaccounted for. Along with FBI agents, Texas Rangers and staff from the medical examiner's office, he sorted through hundreds of bones, which they first had to excavate from under the rubble and unexploded ordnance. He and Owsley were part of the team that then listed probable ages and sexes and matched what they could with skeletal x-rays. Keeping their minds open to any and all possibilities was essential.

Such work affects a forensic anthropologist's personal life. Investigations and testifying at trials mean time away from home. Even at home the work intrudes. At Ubelaker's Christmas tree farm in Virginia, he pokes scraps of plastic and other compounds into fires, just to see how they'll emerge. Burned drywall, it turns out, can resemble bone. So can garden hose.

"You do develop a special interest in tire irons," he adds. "I can't go into an auto supply store without evaluating the differences between them."

Promoting Accuracy in Mysteries

Sometimes, fiction overtakes fact in the museum's anthropology department. Best-selling crime novelist Patricia Cornwell consulted with Ubelaker as she worked on All That Remains, about a serial killer in Virginia. Cornwell spent a day with Ubelaker, looking at slides of damaged bones and trying to figure out what cut marks on a hand phalanx, a finger bone, would look like. "I asked him what a serrated knife would do," Cornwell says. "Doug told me that with a slice it's impossible to tell, because the points of the blade would cover their own tracks. Only if the bone was hacked could you tell." In her book, the heroine--Kay Scarpetta, a medical examiner--is able to determine that a bone has been hacked, a wound incurred when the victim tried to defend herself. And Ubelaker was the inspiration for the character Dr. Alex Vessey, the Smithsonian's expert bone man.

Nursing Home Man, after several hours on the table, smells warm and mammally. His bones feel greasy, which isn't unpleasant, but they're also flecked with bits of dried tissue and a waxy, light brown substance--adipocere, a byproduct of fat decomposition in moist conditions. Owsley isn't wearing gloves, so I make up my mind to be brave, as well. In grad school, Owsley was assigned to work on an extremely fat woman who was found dead and in an advanced state of decomposition in the Smoky Mountains. Her body, says Owsley, was actually foaming with adipocere, and the odor was intense. "I worked for ten minutes, threw up for ten minutes, worked for ten minutes, threw up for ten." And then he never threw up again.

Owsley now looks for any "inclusions" in the cardboard box--bullets, rings, documents, a shoe. Save for the rabbit bone, the box contains only human parts. He notes taphonomic evidence, that is, any changes that affected the body after death. Such evidence may include vegetation that grew on a body as it lay under a porch, silt that settled in bone cracks when the skeleton was later dragged toward a river, a snail shell that lodged between vertebrae as the spine drifted downstream. "One of the great things about the Smithsonian," says Owsley, "is that I can pick up the phone and call a botanist to analyze the algae, a geologist for the silt and an invertebrate zoologist for the snail. Forensic anthropology combines a lot of disciplines."

Owsley holds a femur in the air. "See that lipping [bony extensions] on the end? Arthritis," he says. I pick up a fingernail from among pelvic bones and move it up to the hand pile. It's long and yellowed and thick, and it gives me more of the creeps than anything else arrayed on the table, even the equine-looking teeth.

As Owsley examines the ribs, I open a yellow envelope that came with the box. It's full of hair. "Hey," I say. "This hair is kind of dark." Owsley stops and looks over.

"No gray?"

"No, and there's plenty of it--for an old guy."

"Well," he says, "he wasn't really an old guy." The plot thickens; Owsley knows more than he is letting on. He continues, "Actually, this guy was 45." I nod. "His wife put him in the nursing home because of his diminishing mental capabilities. They suspect she was poisoning him, perhaps even while he was in the nursing home."

Now I know that we aren't looking at an elderly man with Alzheimer's who'd wandered away, gotten lost in the woods and died of a heart attack, exposure or starvation. The bones, come to think of it, do look pretty strong, despite the arthritis. Owsley tells me that toxicologists will be working up his bone marrow, looking for evidence of poisoning. Still, he's got to examine each bone for signs of trauma. Had the dead man been in a fistfight? The nose does not appear broken. The hyoid, a fragile bone in the throat, is intact, but strangulation can't be ruled out. Had he battled an attacker? The ulna--one of the forearm bones, a common spot for a parry fracture-- shows no sign of trauma. Nor do the ribs, all 23 of them. Without a major bullet hole to offer immediate gratification, I can imagine this inventory becoming tedious. But Owsley doesn't let up. "You have to go all out on each case," he says. "Each person is equally important. Someone cared about him."

Sometimes, the person who cares doesn't get satisfaction for a long, long time. In January of 1978, in a small Midwestern town, the trailer home of a family named Morris caught fire. Mrs. Morris reported that there had been an explosion and that her husband had rescued her 5-year-old son from the flames, and a neighbor had rescued her 9-year-old. Her husband, Donald Morris, she said, threw her out of the trailer, then attempted to rescue her 5-year-old. But the two never made it out. The fire chief, brand-new on the job, ruled out arson. The medical examiner declared the deaths accidental and did not perform autopsies.

Morris' brother, however, told the chief of detectives that the entire case smelled fishy to him. Dan D'Annunzio, the newest detective on the staff, was assigned to the case. D'Annunzio brought in one arson investigator who said the fire had been set. A second expert concurred. D'Annunzio asked to have the bodies exhumed, but the medical examiner refused.

For the next 15 years D'Annunzio worked on the case whenever time allowed. In 1993 he thought he had enough to reopen the case. The county attorney told him that if he could come up with one more piece of evidence, he would do it. D'Annunzio then found the older son in a prison. The son told him that he had woken that winter night and seen his mother hit his stepfather over the head with an ashtray and then stab him repeatedly in the back as he lay on the floor.

From a high shelf in the hall, Owsley retrieves Donald Morris, neatly arranged among crisp white sheets in a large cardboard box. Owsley sits cross-legged on the floor and takes out the bones. Morris' skull is badly burned, covered with dry patches of black and white that resemble lichen. Owsley holds up a femur. "This case really talks to you. Look at how strong he was--you can see where the hamstrings were attached. Powerful man; you can just imagine him throwing his wife out the window." "Now look at this vertebra." He holds up another one. "See the cut mark?" I do: there's an angular end on the transverse process (an extension to the side) of this lumbar vertebra. I can see the sharp cuts of a knife or machete. Owsley shows me several ribs with the same markings, clear evidence of multiple stab wounds.

"This skeleton says so much," Owsley says, again. He's excited now, remembering the case, holding up bones left and right. "Look at the pelvis--it was cracked and then healed. Look at the nose, it's been broken. When I met Morris' brother in the courtroom, he said, 'It's just like Donald is here--you know so much about him.'" Partly on the basis of Owsley's work, a jury convicted Mrs. Morris of two counts of murder and one of arson.

Precisely because Morris' skeleton was so expressive, Owsley asked the family if the Smithsonian could have it for its collections, to use for teaching. They agreed.

That case was closed. Nursing Home Man was proving more intractable. Owsley finished examining the remains. He found no evidence of trauma, and the toxicologists found not a trace of poison in his bone marrow. The man's wife may have committed the perfect crime, but it's still too soon to tell. Owsley has started on another dozen cases--an unidentified skeleton from Northern Virginia, a young girl with cut marks on her cervical vertebrae--but he hasn't closed the book on Nursing Home Man quite yet. He's got a more powerful microscope down the hall, and he plans to look at each of the 205 bones once again.

Elizabeth Royte lives in New York City. She writes about the natural world for Outside, the New York Times Magazine, Harpers and other periodicals.

4

Military Lab Puts Name on a Long-Lost Airman

Michael Wilson

The melting snow of the Sierra Nevada fell away from the airman inch by inch. He lay facedown, his hair thick and blond atop a crushed head.

Last October, two hikers on the Darwin Glacier in California spotted a piece of cloth, moved closer and found him. His arms were spread as if in free fall. The parachute pack on his back read "U.S. Army," and it was unopened.

A military team arrived to cut him out, ice and all, and transported him to a remote laboratory at Hickam Air Force Base on Oahu, where anthropologists gently thawed him by spraying him with water.

A mummified human time capsule took its broken shape before them. He carried a Sheaffer fountain pen. The newest coin in his pocket was dated 1942. But his nameplate was terribly corroded, and so the case of the frozen airman took its place among thousands of unidentified remains boxed on crowded shelves or spread on metal tables here at the Joint P.O.W./M.I.A. Accounting Command.

On Friday, the World War II airman will be laid to rest in a private ceremony in his hometown, Brainerd, Minn., after teams of anthropologists and historians here pieced together his identity as the missing crew member from a plane crash 63 years ago. His journey from the snow to the laboratory to the grave fulfills what a commander here describes as the military's "most sacred of promises" to its members.

"We're going back to that basic promise we make to youngsters who enter the military," said Col. Claude H. Davis III of the Marines, deputy commander of the joint command, which is dedicated to finding and identifying the remains of Americans from all wars. "We're going to make sure they get home again."

An estimated 88,000 military personnel remain unaccounted for, a vast majority, 78,000, from World War II, and most of those are believed to be lost at sea.

About 8,100 service members remain missing from the Korean War; from Vietnam, 1,807. There are 126 military or intelligence officers missing from the cold war, mostly in spy planes that crashed. Some of the missing are civilians like Red Cross workers and C.I.A. agents, and some, like the frozen airman, went missing here in the United States.

The work is slow going. The 425-member staff of the accounting command identifies an average of six people a month, about 75 a year, each one ending with a flag-draped return to a family, often distant relatives.

"It's not like you're just working on a bunch of bones," Johnie E. Webb, 60, the senior adviser, said. "It's very rewarding. It's also very agonizing. Family members are getting older."

The laboratory is part cutting edge, part time warp. A computer can superimpose the image of an unidentified skull over a man's smiling picture, a haunting montage of optimism and fate, to see whether the eye sockets and teeth match up.

A bone sample the size of a thumb can yield mitochondrial DNA to link a man missing 60 years to a child in short pants.

Books about old military buttons and medals and knives line the walls. Broken stopwatches mark the time of long-ago crashes.

The command operates on an annual budget of $45 million to $50 million. The front end of the process, finding the remains, is expensive and often time consuming, involving linguists, investigators and hours spent developing leads and studying flight plans or battle reports.

Eighteen recovery teams of up to 14 members make several 35-day missions a year to Southeast Asia, Korea, Europe and the Pacific theater of World War II.

The easy cases are already closed.

"All the apples pretty close to the tree are gone," said Robert Richeson, deputy director of the section that oversees investigations. "The crash sites we get to these days are a little tougher to do."

In "isolated grave" cases, where an individual has been buried or left on a battlefield, the rate of recovery and identification is 17 percent of all sites investigated, Mr. Richeson said.

A stroll through the vault of remains shows where extractions were successful: Belgium, Burma, Cambodia, France, Laos, Papua and North and South Korea.

None of the remains in the boxes have been identified, and the frustration of the families of the dead runs deep. An old letter in a file from the mother of a missing Korean War soldier reads: "I guess the search party didn't do a good job. I wish I was there. I would of dug every inch of that ground myself."

Most crash-site investigations begin just as the airman's did, with someone happening upon it. After the hikers' discovery on Oct. 15, which generated widespread interest and news coverage, historians with the command turned to accident reports from the 1940's, in hopes of finding a match in the Sierra Nevada.

There it was. On the morning of Nov. 18, 1942, three young aviation cadets and a pilot took off from Mather Field, near Sacramento, for a four-hour navigational training flight. The airplane carried five hours' worth of fuel and never returned. The searchers -- military crews, police officers, loggers and local residents -- found nothing.

Almost five years later, two college students found parts of the airplane, a nametag belonging to one of the men and what a search team's report described as "a small piece of frozen flesh." The remains were interred in a group burial in San Bruno, Calif., that bore the names of all four men.

If the frozen airman was one of the men, which one? His features were long ago obliterated by the elements.

"Even examining his body there on the autopsy table," Robert Mann, deputy scientific director at the command, said, "it was difficult to tell what we were looking at."

One leg was gone. There was no face, only deep holes in a dark mass. He had lost six teeth while alive, their sockets long ago healed, and one tooth at his death. The blond hair fell to the right, in the style of the day.

Most recoveries involve, at best, skeletons, the dirt around them slowly cleared with trowels and brushes. But more often there are just jagged pieces of bone no larger than a bullet, and even those are hard won.

"Every one's a new challenge," said Gregory Fox, 54, an archaeologist who works on several recovery missions a year. "You're on a 60-foot slope this time or a cliff or you're diverting a stream."

Often, they find nothing.

"I went on two missions without finding anything," Capt. Loren Graham, 34, a recovery team leader, said. "That's 60 days. We found buckets and buckets, but we didn't find any bone and we didn't find any teeth."

In Southeast Asia, many crash sites were long ago picked over by looters. Some cases begin when a son or daughter in Vietnam or Laos finds American dog tags among a dead parent's possessions and takes them to the authorities.

On April 7, 2001, a command helicopter carrying a team searching for remains crashed in Quang Binh Province in Vietnam, killing all seven Americans and nine Vietnamese on board. A memorial stands outside the command office near Pearl Harbor.

Digging out the airman in the Sierra was relatively easy. At the laboratory, scientists picked through his modest personal effects - - a broken comb, the pen, six pennies, one nickel, four dimes, three address books that were illegible.

Most unusual was a scrap of paper that they fed into a high-resolution video spectral comparator, discovering what appears to be a bawdy limerick that read in part, "A bird in the hand is worth two in the bush, this the girls all know." The parachute on his back was intact. Spread on the asphalt outside, it even looked usable.

Finally, the corroded nameplate. Anthropologists used different sources of light to photograph the plate until teasing four letters from the scarred metal: "EO A. M."

One of the dead men was listed as Leo M. Mustonen, age 22. Close to the nameplate, but with a different middle initial. His death report listed his emergency contacts as his parents, Arvid and Anna Mustonen, Finnish immigrants on Maple Street in Brainerd, Minn.

A piece of bone generated mitochondrial DNA, but for a successful match, a sample has to be drawn from a maternal relative. The lone relatives of the airman named Mustonen were the wife and daughters of his brother, in Jacksonville, Fla. Their DNA would not be of help.

But relatives of the other three missing airmen -- John Mortenson, 25, of Idaho; Ernest Munn, 23, of Ohio; and the pilot, Second Lt. William Gamber, 23, also of Ohio -- were found. None matched the frozen airman's DNA.

Finally, anthropologists found that Mustonen's name had been misspelled on his nameplate all along. The A should have been M.

So by the nametag and genetic default, and "to the exclusion of other reasonable possibilities," the airman was identified as Leo M. Mustonen. Formal notification was made to Leane Mustonen Ross in Jacksonville, who was not born when the airplane carrying her father's brother crashed.

His remains were cremated and shipped to Minnesota.

Ms. Ross said imagining her uncle's final moments haunted her.

"He actually made it out of the plane," she said. "Then, the parachute didn't open. He might not have had enough altitude to open his parachute."

She said she knew of three people alive who had known her uncle, and she planned the funeral for Friday at the First Lutheran Church in Brainerd. A military team will perform taps and fire a 21-gun salute.

A picture of the mummified airman is in Ms. Ross's house, in a report from the command, but she said she would not look. She prefers the high school picture of her uncle when he was 18, a member of a school band, his young face stern, his blond hair swept to the right.

Part 2

Crime Scene Photography

1

Picture an Investigation

Crime Scene Photography

David W. MacKenna

Sometimes a picture is worth far more than a thousand words. In corporate investigations of accidents or crimes, photography can help record the scene, define the cause of a problem, and possibly identify a suspect.

Shortly after photography's origin, police agencies in major European cities used photographs to record the physical features of criminal suspects. Not to be outdone, US police and prosecutors in the early 1860s began to use photographs as evidence in criminal trials.

Through the years, photography has held an increasingly important place in public and private law enforcement with applications in criminal identification, surveillance, and crime scene and laboratory evidence examination. In fact, special cameras can now be attached to electron microscopes and comparison microscopes for laboratory analysis of blood, hair, fibers, and other trace evidence found at scenes or taken directly from suspects.

Because of photography's potential for improving the quality of criminal investigations, all security departments should have suitable camera equipment on hand. Security officers, especially those with direct investigative responsibilities, should be trained in the effective use of such equipment at incident scenes.

Basically, photographs are taken at a crime scene to show what has occurred. If the incident involves criminal activity, photographs may aid in suspect identification or, if the case reaches the courtroom, may support testimony.

Every incident scene poses unique investigative problems. A vehicle accident is not just another car crash. A burglary is not just another breaking and entering. Even when security officers confront

Picture an Investigation by David W. MacKenna. (c) 1990 ASIS International, 1625 Prince Street, Alexandria, VA 22314. Reprinted with permission from the August 1990 issue of Security Management magazine.

related or serial incidents, evidence always varies. Therefore, investigators must never approach a crime scene casually or they risk overlooking information that might identify the suspect or clarify what has taken place. Well-planned, well-executed photographs are essential to thorough search and analysis of crime scenes.

For accurate crime scene photography, the investigator must not add to or subtract from the scene or move or handle any items found there. Conditions should be photographed just as they are. In addition, the investigator should shoot an overall or general view, a mid-range relationship view, and a close-up view of specific evidence.

Any photograph is better than none at all. Consequently, a small security department could begin by buying an instant film camera of the type manufactured by Polaroid Corporation. The obvious advantage of these cameras is the opportunity to view results within seconds and reshoot if the quality is unsatisfactory. Also, little skill is required for instant photography under normal lighting conditions. Even though the instant process does not produce negatives, photographs can be reproduced or enlarged in the laboratory.

Of course, for evidence it is always important to retain the original photograph. Some investigators who use large format or 35 mm equipment also take preliminary instant shots as insurance against the possibility of camera or darkroom error.

A second equipment option is instamatic cameras, which use either I 10 or 126 film. Such equipment is inexpensive to use and easy to operate; however, its quality is unsuitable for crime scene use. Instamatics have fixed-focus lens systems that present objects in focus between about 4 ft. and infinity. Most such cameras cannot be adjusted; you simply point the camera and shoot. In addition, I 10 film is difficult to work with in the darkroom because of its small size.

The 126 camera has increased in popularity over the years, largely because it is simple to load and operate. Modem plastic film cartridges can be inserted in the camera with no need to thread or touch the film. These cameras are available in a wide range of prices and styles, but even the most expensive models lack the necessary versatility for incident or crime scene applications.

Historically, there have been two primary schools of thought on the best equipment for investigative use. Some people have advocated cameras that provide large negatives (a minimum o 21/4" x 21/4"), contending that such negatives provide greater print quality in the enlarging process. A second group has favored 35 mm equipment.

One type of 21/4-in. format camera, the twin-lens reflex (TLR), uses 120 film. TLRs have two optical systems, one of which projects to the film under shutter control. The other presents the image upward for viewing on a ground glass screen. Because the systems are linked, correct focus is assured. Also on the market are 21/4-in. single-lens reflex (SLR) cameras, similar to traditional 35 mm equipment. Both models have the advantage of larger negatives but tend to be heavy and expensive.

Another large format model that meets investigative requirements in most applications is the 4" x 5" camera. Such a camera is versatile, dependable, and not overly expensive. It can even be converted to Polaroid use with an adaptable film pack. The system can also be converted to mug shot applications or used as an excellent fingerprint camera. A 4" x 5" negative permits sizable enlargement with minimal loss of clarity.

In the past, 4" x 5' cameras were popular with journalists and police photographers. At present, however, improvements in equipment and film have made 35 nun cameras the dominant type for press and investigative applications. Smaller camera size, removable lenses, high-speed film, fast shutter speeds, microprocessor circuitry, and low cost have contributed to the popularity of 35 mm systems. The primary disadvantage is a relatively small negative, but it can be enlarged with satisfactory clarity to an 8' x 10" print. Rarely are larger prints required for investigative or courtroom purposes.

During the past decade video cameras have become increasingly popular for such security applications as incident and crime scene photography. Stationary video cameras have long been used in monitoring and surveillance applications, but modem portable equipment can effectively record witness testimony, lineups, or conditions at crime, vehicle, or industrial accident scenes. Nevertheless, many investigators still prefer the ease and speed of still photography, which produces single photographs that can readily be displayed and attached to reports.

Whether still or video, a camera's lens captures light from the image and directs it to the film. Security investigators confronted with varying photographic requirements at incident scenes may need to change lenses to maximize a camera's effectiveness.

Basically, lenses come in three categories: normal, wide-angle, and telephoto. Photographers consider a normal lens to be one with a focal length equal to the diagonal measure of the image area. For a 35 mm camera, then, the normal lens is 50 mm. A lens of this size is usually standard equipment on cameras with removable lens systems. Security personnel who photograph accidents or crime scenes will find a normal lens appropriate for most situations.

A wide-angle lens has a shorter focal length than a normal one and covers a viewing angle of about 60 degrees, in contrast to the 45 degree angle of a 50 mm lens. For 35 mm cameras, several wide-angle sizes are on the market, the most popular of which are 28 mm and 35 mm. Wide-angle shots are especially effective in depicting buildings in relation to other objects, interior rooms when it is necessary to illustrate relative position of several evidentiary items, and general panoramic exterior scenes.

A longer focal length or telephoto lens provides a close-up view of distant objects. Thus, a 100 mm lens illustrates twice the detail of a 50 mm lens by presenting less overall area. For identification shots in security, a lens in the 85 mm to 135 mm range is a good choice.

In some instances a telephoto lens may be useful for depicting small items. It is, however, generally less useful than the lens sizes previously described. The primary difficulty in using a telephoto lens is picture blurring due to camera movement or shallow depth of field. To minimize such blurring, for lens sizes above 100 mm, a shutter speed Of /125 second or higher is best if the camera is to be hand-held.

No single camera type serves all security applications. Therefore, the best approach to buying equipment is to prepare personnel for the most common photographic situations. It is also important to standardize equipment as much as possible to reduce the need for duplicate lenses and other accessories, as well as promote general familiarity with cameras on hand.

Two issues that frequently confront organizations as they initiate photographic service are whether to establish an in-house developing and printing capability and whether to shoot black-and-white or color. As a general rule, small security units do not have the picture volume to justify a darkroom, print room, and laboratory equipment. Excellent commercial services are readily available in most locations. Sharing a local police laboratory is yet another way to promote cooperation between security and the police. The issue of color versus black-and-white photography should present little difficulty if commercial labs are used. The general popularity of color has had its effect on law enforcement and security photography in recent years. Thus, security managers should purchase equipment capable of good black-and-white as well as color photography and leave film development to the professionals.

Poorly planned and executed photographs reflect on the general quality of a criminal investigation and may directly affect its outcome. Both video and still photography must meet certain qualifications to be acceptable as courtroom evidence.

First, all such material must be relevant and accurately depict the scene or object photographed. In addition, the subject matter must be clearly identifiable in the picture. In court, questions may also be raised about the photographer's qualifications and experience, the type of camera equipment and film, the conditions under which the photographs or videotapes were made, and the evidentiary chain of custody. The basic purpose of photography in investigations is to present an incident story in visual form. Thus the scene should be undisturbed, to the extent possible, before photographs are taken. As a general guideline, the photographs should progress from the general to the specific. Shots can, therefore, be classified as long-range, mid-range, and close-up. The photographer should think of how the perpetrator entered the scene, committed the act, and exited the scene. With that approach, security managers or investigators can present a series of photographs, in progression, of how the crime occurred.

If portable videotape equipment is used, the investigator should film evidence at the point of discovery and record the date and time it was found and the identity of the person who located it. Just as with still photography, an initial sequence should place the building or scene in relation to surrounding structures. Thus, the standard taping procedure would begin with a distant shot, moving to mid-range and finally close-up views of specific evidentiary items. In videotaping, narration can be a big plus. If the narration is done by someone other than the photographer, the various video sequences must be planned. Except for narration, other aspects of the video process follow the general rules of still photography. The investigator must recognize that photographic completeness is more important than film cost. If the value of a particular shot is in doubt, he or she should take it anyway. It is painful to discover the importance of an untaken photograph or tape sequence after the crime scene has been returned to its normal state.

To present size and distance relationships, the photographer may want to include a ruler or other appropriate measuring device when photographing evidence. Because such devices can clutter photographs, it is accepted practice first to photograph the item or scene in an as-is condition, then to take pictures with rulers or other identification markers in the scene.

Since most crimes require a number of shots at the scene, investigators should also record the chronology of pictures taken as well as the relevant technical and descriptive data relating to each photograph. Such information establishes the how, when, and where of the photographic operation and equips the investigator to describe each picture later in a thorough and professional fashion. The record should be maintained in a photographic log and include at least the following data:

* photographer's name
* date and time of photograph
* nature and location of the incident
* type of camera and film
* light source and environmental conditions
* distance from subject
* shutter speed, aperture setting, and lens focal length

Each original negative and photograph should be retained and treated in the same protective manner as other physical evidence.

Existing room lighting may be satisfactory, especially if fast film is used, but additional illumination may be needed. Photoflood, photoflash, or dedicated electronic flash can provide supplemental lighting; the choice depends on the camera equipment used.

For general views at an incident scene, the photographer should hold the camera at eye level to illustrate conditions as seen by an observer. Naturally, small objects with evidentiary value may require close shots from varying angles.

Each scene has unique features that suggest an appropriate array of pictures to take. Essentially, the goal is to establish the elements of the offense. The following crime and incident summaries outline some photographic subjects that, if captured on film, can prove helpful in an investigation.

Vandalism, illegal entry, and burglary:

* the building exterior in relation to other structures, parking areas, or streets
* suspected points of entry and exit
* specific damage to the structure, equipment, or furnishings
* the general condition of interior rooms or offices entered or damaged by the intruder
* articles or evidence left at the scene, such as tools, tire prints, footprints, or fingerprints
* the specific area from which articles or money was taken (safe or desk)

Fire or possible arson:

* the scene before fire personnel begin to extinguish the fire
* the fire as it progresses

* telephoto shots from some distance, especially if the heat is intense and the fire is confined to one area of a large structure
* burning structures in relation to other nearby buildings
* as many spectators as possible; arsonists frequently watch their fires
* exterior views from various angles after the fire is extinguished (if possible, shots from above, perhaps from adjacent structures)
* interior rooms illustrating fire, smoke, or explosive damage before cleanup
* clocks that are stopped
* shots of windows or doors that suggest possible forced entry
* the suspected point of origin of the fire (in close-up)
* the interior, with both wide-angle and standard lenses

Explosion:

* the source of the explosion (fuel containers, faulty gas lines, open gas valves, ruptured pipes) and any damage caused
* evidence that may indicate the nature of the explosive device, if the explosion is deemed intentional
* any trace evidence, such as bomb container fragments, wire, tape, or batteries
* undetonated parts of a bomb (these may be found some distance from the point of explosion)
* ground zero

Traffic accidents:

* all possible factors that bear on the cause and result of the incident
* the approach of each driver, especially any obstructions to clear view by drivers
* an overall view, as well as four directional shots (north, east, south, and west)
* views from the eye level of each driver, including the point of impact, 25 ft. from that point, and 100 ft. from it
* specific damage to each vehicle, including accident debris to suggest the probable point of impact
* the license plate of each vehicle
* tire and skid marks
* trace evidence, especially in hit-and-run accidents

The primary point to remember about photography in an investigation is that finished products must depict evidence or scene conditions as accurately as possible. A quality photograph must be factual, with minimal distortion. Good photography requires practice, proper equipment, and a clear understanding of fundamentals.

Advances in photographic equipment and technique continually enhance the value of cameras to the security field. Polaroid film is now available in a range of sizes, down to 35 mm. The darkroom as we know it today may all but disappear in the future. Film of higher quality and speed is also being developed. Videotaping is rapidly expanding in security and law enforcement applications. But in the future, still photography will continue as a vital part of security investigations.

About the Author: David W. MacKenna, CPP, is an associate professor of criminal justice at the University of Texas at Arlington. A former special agent with the US Air Force Office of Special Investigations, he teaches criminal investigation and security. He is a member of ASIS.

2

New Forensic Photography Methods Help Identify, Solve Crimes

Megan Christensen

If you take your last breath in Wayne County, Mich., you should hope your corpse won't come into contact with Joseph Sopkowicz and Bobbie Gary.

Because that would mean you are among the nameless dead, without family or friends, without fingerprints on file, without links to the usual databases, dental records or X rays that are often used to identify bodies.

Your body will be in cold storage, perhaps for months, while investigators do their best to identify you before you are laid to rest.

Some might say that handling photos from death scenes and autopsies is a gruesome job.

Sopkowicz, a forensic photographer, would disagree.

"It has a positive end to it if we can help solve a crime or find out who these people are," he said. Sopkowicz creates photos that often offer the only link to the identity of a nameless body.

Using a computer, he manipulates autopsy photos to re-create each person as he or she may have looked. He pulls up a file with dozens of eye shapes and then superimposes the best match on the face. He colors the irises and, suddenly, the dead gaze out from the screen.

A few more mouse-clicks paint on clothing and warm the skin to natural tones. He plays with the details until they feel real to him.

"Zooming in on the unknown dead: New methods help identify, solve crimes" by Megan Christensen from THE DETROIT FREE PRESS, July 8, 2003. Reprinted by permission of the Detroit Free Press.

If possible, Sopkowicz edits the photos to show distinctive teeth. No one would mistake the look for a smile, but it aids identification.

Gary, an investigator, was a Detroit homicide detective for 12 years. Five years ago, he retired after 27 years on the force and joined the medical examiner's team.

"It's just like when I was working in homicide," he said. "You want to close your cases."

The morgue's 15 investigators process more than 12,000 deaths each year. Most cases are routine paperwork; only about 3,300 bodies actually come through the morgue. Many bodies spend a few hours in anonymity before anxious families claim them, but a handful of cases go unsolved, the paperwork at a dead end and the bodies in frozen storage.

Gary has four troublesome cases this summer. Out of 96 unidentified people at the morgue since January, two still have no names. Two more cases linger from last year.

They include a young woman abandoned in an alley after an overdose; a Jane Doe struck by a Corvette; a woman in her 60s who slept on porches, and a man huddled in an abandoned foot clinic.

Consider Case No. 11355: On Nov. 30, two young boys found a woman naked from the waist down in an alley. Her body was cold and dusted with snow. Scrapes marked her chin, knees and elbows. She died of a cocaine overdose.

The medical examiners placed her age at between 25 and 30. She is black, 5-feet-5, 121 pounds. She may have been a prostitute who went by the nickname Starr.

She didn't die in the alley, Gary said.

"Most likely, she was in a dope house and OD'd. People get scared, they wait until the middle of the night, or until they get their courage up, and they drop them somewhere," he said.

Case No. 02-03432 also is still open. In April 2002, a hit-and-run driver left a woman in the street. A red Corvette sped away, and the victim died at a Detroit hospital.

Clerks in neighborhood stores said she was homeless and returned to the area each spring. She is black, in her 60s, dressed in a black shearling coat. She is 5-feet-6, 215 pounds, with medium-length black hair.

The woman known as No. 03-05400 died last month. Neighbors noticed her sleeping on a porch in Highland Park, Mich., for several days. When she disappeared, residents called police, but they never knew her name.

She is white, in her 60s, 5-feet-6, 129 pounds, with graying medium-length hair. She wore two pairs of jeans and three sweatshirts.

"Highland Park is predominantly black," Gary noted. "You would not expect to find her there in that neighborhood."

Police found John Doe No. 03-02266 on March 5. The man, age 45-50, with sandy hair, died of heart disease in an abandoned podiatrist's office. He wore jeans, a green long-sleeve shirt, a vest, a camouflage jacket, one white gym shoe and a pair of battery-powered socks.

When all else fails and investigators have exhausted every lead, the county buries the dead and files all known details _ in case someone comes looking in the future.

Part 3

Offender Profiling

1

Offender Profiling

Estimation or Guesstimation?

Sandie Taylor

I t is difficult to turn on a television or go to the cinema without
coming across a fictional portrayal of a serial murderer being
tracked by a team of investigators assisted by a brilliant
psychologist. Popular films such as Silence of the Lambs and
television shows like Cracker, Wire in the Blood and Walking the
Dead often depict offender profiling in dramatic fashion. But that is
the movies--can it rally be done to such precision in real life?

Offender profiling is not a new concept. Its roots call be
traced back to the nineteenth century, when the study of individual
differences was very much in vogue. Sir Francis Galton (1822-1911),
for instance, spent much of his time researching the link between
body size and intellectual functioning. Franz Joseph Gall (1758-1828)
used the 'science' of phrenology--the method of interpreting
personality characteristics based on the size and shape of bumps on
the head.

Offender profiling draws upon implicit knowledge of
personality and utilises the statistical methods typically adopted by
personality researchers (psychometric testing and multi-dimensional
scaling). Computer programs have been developed to deal with the
nature of data collection used by profilers and have played a major
role in police investigation. But what exactly is offender profiling?

What is offender profiling?

Offender profiling is defined by Geberth (1981) as 'An educated
attempt to provide investigative agencies with specific information as
to the type of individual who committed a certain crime.'

Clearly, Geberth makes to attempt to disguise offender
profiling as a scientifically foolproof method of working. He is

Offender Profiling: Estimation or Guesstimation? by Sandie Taylor
from PSYCHOLOGY REVIEW (2004), Vol.11(2), pp. 20-25.

further quoted as saying in a personal communication to Holmes and Holmes (1996), 'Criminal profiling is an excellent law enforcement tool. However, it is just one of many tools and does not replace good investigative techniques.'

Offender profiling is best applied to certain types of crime (lust and mutilation murders; rapes; motiveless fire setting; postmortem slashing and cutting; evisceration; sadistic torture in sexual assaults and satanic and cult murders) and to cases where there have been multiple attempts. These crimes reflect pathology in the offender and it is this knowledge that offender profilers rely upon. Additionally, profilers offer insight from the evidence at the crime scene as to the nature of the pathology manifested through the crime.

When considering different crimes, investigators use a hierarchical template of decision making. For instance, the obvious questions are: what class of crime (property or person oriented), what type of crime (robbery or rape), what criminal actions occurred and what method of criminal operation was in use? In other words, what were the modus operandi? Such information helps profilers to develop a criminal signature.

One way of understanding the concept of a criminal signature is to consider the following case of the American Edmund Kempler. Since the young age of ten, Kempler had had fantasies of killing his mother using a hammer. It took the killings of ten other people, using a hammer, before he succumbed to murdering his mother. His fantasies took over and became more and more elaborate until he mutilated and dismembered his victims, had necrophilic relationships with them and disposed of their body parts in his mother's house. The sheer escalation of his fantasies meant that he became less careful and therefore vulnerable to capture.

Another example is William Heirens, known as the Boston strangler, who would pose as a utility man with a forged identity badge. He also had the gift of the gab and talked his way into women's homes, where he would then strangle them using their own tights. In both of these cases, profilers can identity a modus operandi and a criminal signature unique to the killer.

Obviously in cases of serial murder, where there are no surviving victims to provide eyewitness testimonial accounts, the crime scene becomes the main source of evidential information.

Assumptions of the profiling process

The crime scene is of paramount importance, as it reflects the personality of the offender. This connection between crime scene and personality is particularly pertinent to the profiling process used in the USA. The theoretical assumption here is that the central core of our personality does not change dramatically in a short space of time. This also applies to criminals and criminal behaviour. A criminal lifestyle does not develop overnight, nor does it change as suddenly. And multiple killing is like an addiction, in that the inherent details of the crime tend to remain constant and are repeated across crime events. It is not only personality characteristics that can be deduced from the crime scene, but the behaviour of the offender during and after the offence, and it is this behaviour which helps investigators decide whether the case is suitable for profiling (Holmes and Holmes 1996).

Analysis of a serial killer's psyche

Despite the diversity of modus operandi and criminal signature displayed by serial killers, Holmes and Holmes (1996) point out that the experience of the process of violence is similar. The model of personal violence proposed by Holmes and Holmes embraces a psychoanalytic stance. It depicts a five-stage process which can be influenced by external forces, whether real or imagined by the perpetrator.

During stage 1 (distorted thinking) the perpetrator is in a positive psychological state, whereby the consequences of his or her deviant thoughts are ignored. This temporary state of psychological equilibrium soon gives way to stage 2 (the fall). There is no return to distorted thinking once the fall has been initiated. It is during this phase that the perpetrator stores incidents, imagined or real, deep within his or her psyche. Often these incidents are perceived by the perpetrator as negative and ego-threatening and are believed to warrant a violent reaction. Stage 3, referred to as the negative inward response, is where the perpetrator must deal with feelings of inadequacy. This he does by confronting negative reality messages and restoring the ego through actions of violence, which are carried out in stage 4. The perpetrator has now progressed from mental preparation to the negative outward response--the act itself. A victim has to be found in order to subdue any more negative reality messages. By stage 5, the perpetrator's status has been restored and concerns are now focused towards victim disposal. This completes the cycle and the perpetrator then returns to stage 1.

The implications of Holmes and Holmes' model of personal violence is twofold. It provides investigators with a time frame of when the killer is likely to strike next. Furthermore, it informs investigators of how the perpetrator's killing career is developing. Often the distorted thinking escalates and the modus operandi, although consistent, becomes more elaborative and bizarre with time and frequency of killing. Killers become careless and it is this that often leads to their capture.

The American serial killer, Jeffrey Dahmer, demonstrates this clearly. Police were alerted by a man called Tracy Edwards, who had managed to escape from the clutches of Dahmer. Edwards explained how he was drugged but awoke to Dahmer's advances. He tried to leave, but Dahmer handcuffed him and made him watch The Exorcist, with a butcher's knife to his chest. Dahmer told Edwards that he was going to kill him, take his heart out and eat it. Edwards took the police to Dahmer's apartment. They were taken aback by its horrible smell and when they questioned Dahmer, he became hysterical and struggled with them. In the apartment the police found human remains in varying stages of decomposition and body parts in his fridge, ready fur eating. This is how the police found out about Dahmer's years of killing. Dahmer became careless, and in so doing, enabled his victim to escape. Furthermore, the time frame between stages 1 and 5 decreased as his killing spree continued. Body disposal was barely successfully concluded before the next killing. The model of personal violence can be very informative in understanding the psyche of a serial killer.

How does offender profiling operate?

There appear to be different approaches to offender profiling which dictate how it is defined and used.

The US experience

The FBI headquarters in Quentico, USA, has a special section known as the Behavioural Sciences Unit. It was here that Ressler developed offender profiling and coined the term 'serial killer'. Ressler's Criminal Personality Research Project started in 1978, during which he interviewed over 100 infamous offenders.

Much information was collected through interviewing offenders, reviewing police files and examining crime scenes. The effort of collating all this information led to a psychological typologies approach--namely the differentiation between organised non-social and disorganised asocial killers. Killers belonging to these two typologies would lead very different lifestyles, have different personality traits, leave very different crime scenes, demonstrate different post-offence behaviour and require different interview tactics from the police (see Box 1). Differences in the personalities of the organised non-social and the disorganised asocial offender should be reflected in the crime scene. Thus those organised in life will be organised in crime, and this is reflected in the meticulous way a crime is planned and carried out. The organised person will leave the crime scene with very little incriminating evidence.

Holmes and DeBurger (1988) have out lined further typologies based on interviews of serial killers incarcerated in US prisons. These include: visionary, missionary, hedonistic (lust or comfort-oriented) and power/control killer (see Box 2 Further typologies defined by Douglas et al. (1992)). Peter Sutcliff is an example of a visionary killer, who claimed he was instructed by God to rid the streets of prostitutes. Killers like Ken Bianchi and Angelo Buno in the USA are examples of lust killers, who tortured their victims through suffocation and prompt resuscitation for the thrill of it. Herman Mudgett, on the other hand, illustrates the comfort-oriented killer who killed his wives, fiancees and employers to gain property and money. Harold Shipman, who watched his vulnerable old patients die by lethal injection, and Myra Hindley and her partner in crime, Ian Brady, who tortured and murdered children, are typical power/ control killers or psychopaths.

Inherent within these typologies is the dimension of spatial mobility, which also features strongly in the British approach. A geographically stable murderer lives in the same area for a substantial period of time, and therefore kills and disposes of bodies in the same area or in a nearby area with which he is familiar. John Gacy, Bible John and Harold Shipman are examples of geographically stable murderers. Geographically transient killers, on the other hand, are constantly travelling to far-ranging areas, as did killers like Ted Bundy and Peter Sutcliff.

The British experience

One of Britain's leading investigative psychologists is David Canter, who has written many books detailing the profiling perspective in Britain today. He has outlined the usefulness of using the Radex model to challenge the over-simplistic American approach of having a limited number of criminal typologies. The application of the Radex model is straightforward. If perceived as a series of concentric circles, the inner circle would hold all actions that typify criminal behaviour and are shared therefore by the majority of criminals. Within the second circle, criminal actions become less generic and more specific to certain types of crimes and modus operandi. Very specific and less frequently encountered criminal actions would be even further away from the inner circle or the core of generic criminality.

In Britain, the emphasis is less on pigeonholing serial killers into one of two categories based on personality typology and more on the notion of behavioural consistency in terms of habits, attitudes to others and skill. Behavioural consistency occurs in criminal behaviour too, as in modus operandi. A modern development used by police investigators is crime analysis, which has been defined as

> The analysis of every crime with every other
> crime and with criminals to identify links that
> are not evident from routine police enquiries.
> In psychological research terms this may be
> translated into the analysis of a set of behaviours
> with other sets of behaviours and the
> individuals who may be responsible.

(Merry 2000, page 302)

The crime analyst utilises information about behaviour derived from the crime scene and information of geographic demography. These two sources of information help us understand how people operate within their geographical area. Crime analysis enables investigators to deduce information from three working models referred to by Merry (2000) as comparative case analysis, suspect identification and target profiling. An abundance of useful information can be obtained about the similarity of modus operandi across similar and non similar crimes. Furthermore, information about the comings and goings of a suspected offender within a specified location can be mapped using multi-dimensional scaling techniques such as smallest space analysis (SSA). Similar mappings can be obtained for suspect identification and target profiling (see Figure 1 for an example of this mapping).

Concluding thoughts

Offender profiling is a useful method of working and, coupled with computer technology, it might prove to be a methodical asset to crime investigators. Perhaps it may also prove useful in helping to solve crimes other than murder. According to Canter and Alison (2000) this has been shown to be true. So we can see that there are differences between the US and British methods of profiling and although the US way may seem more exciting, it has not been without criticism.

Key concepts

* Definition of offender profiling
* Offender pathology
* Hierarchical template of decision making
* Criminal signature/modus operandi

* Model of personal violence (Holmes and Holmes)
* Psychological typologies approach
* Spatial mobility
* Radex model
* Crime analysis
* Three working models (Merry)

Box 1 Psychological typologies

Organised non-social	Disorganised asocial
Personal characteristics	Personal characteristics
Socially adequate	Socially inadequate
Sexually competent	Sexually inadequate
Controlled mood	Anxious mood during criminal activity
Charming	Poor hygiene
Model prisoner	
Geographically/occupationally mobile	Lives and works near crime scene
Follows media	
Egotist	
Masculine image	
High IQ	Low IQ
High birth order	
Lives with partner	Lives alone
	Significant behavioural change
	Secret hiding place
	Unskilled work
	Nocturnal
Post-offence behaviour	Post-offence behaviour
Returns to crime scene	Returns to crime scene to relive event
Volunteers information	Attends funeral, places a memoriam
May move the body	
May dispose of the body to advertise crime	
Police groupies	Keeps diary/news cuttings of events
Anticipates questioning	
	May change abode, job and personality
Interview techniques	Interview techniques
Use direct strategy	Empathise with offender

Use counsellor approach
Must be certain of details   Indirectly introduce evidence
Offenders will admit only what
  they have to
                        Night-time interview

Box 2 Further typologies defined by Douglas et al. (1992)

Typology	Mental state	Method
Visionary serial killers	Psychotic: hear voices and see visions propelling them to kill	Little crime scene planning, quick kill (act focused)
Missionary serial killers	Not psychotic, self imposed duty to eradicate a specific class of people	Act focused, organised or disorganised
Hedonistic serial killers		
I Lust or thrill	Make connection between personal violence and sexual gratification, pleasure derived from killing	Killing is long drawn out process (process focused), involves domination, torture, fear instilling
II Comfort-oriented	Make connection between killing and obtaining personal gain	act focused
III Power/control serial killers	Psychopath, make connection between sexual gratification and domination over victim, pleasure derived from power and control	Process focused

References

Canter, D. and Alison, L. (2000) Profiling Property Crimes. Offender Profiling Series, Vol. 4, Ashgate Dartmouth.

Geberth, V. (1981) 'Psychological profiling', Law and Order, No. 29, pp. 46-49.

Holmes, R. M. and DeBurger, J. (1988) 'Profiles in Terror: the serial murderer', in R. M. Holmes and S. T. Holmes (eds) (1996) Profiling Violent Crimes. An Investigative Tool, Sage Publications.

Holmes, R. M. and Holmes, S. T. (1996) Profiling Violent Crimes: An Investigative Tool, Sage Publications.

Merry, S. (2000) 'Crime analysis: principles for analysing everyday serial crime', in D. Canter and L. Alison (eds) Profiling Property Crimes. Offender Profiling Series, Vol. 4, Ashgate Dartmouth.

Sandie Taylor is a Senior Lecturer at Bath Spa University College. Her research interests include areas within criminological and investigative psychology, face recognition and human lateralisation for emotions. She currently supervises research on mock juror decision making and lateralisation for language.

Part 4

Ballistics

1

New Tagging Technique for Bullets Shoots Holes in "Fingerprinting"

Amy Higgins, Sherri Koucky

Ballistic fingerprinting has its critics. Used for years, it involves analyzing the unique markings of fired bullets and empty shell casings and then matching them to specific firearms. Proponents say ballistic studies help law officers match guns with crime-scene evidence. Critics, on the other hand, claim the technique is just a way to register and eventually confiscate all lawfully owned handguns. They also say ballistic markings can be easily altered, essentially making the "fingerprints" useless.

One company aims to change that with an alternative tagging technology said to be proof positive. NanoVia LP, Londonderry, N.H. (www.nanovia.com), has developed a microembossing technique that stamps each cartridge casing as bullets fire. The microscopic code can be made up of encrypted symbols, bar codes, or simple alphanumeric codes, such as the make, model, and tracking number. Manufacturers can access the code to find out a firearm's serial number and purchasing history. The company says these identifiers, called NanoTag Ballistic ID Tags, would immediately lead investigators to a specific gun without requiring the extra manpower and expense associated with trying to match "scratches and dings" that can be easily altered. The technique uses imaging equipment found in local, state, and federal forensics labs.

NanoVia is working with the State of California Department of Justice to test various code configurations and to see where the embossing surfaces should sit within the firearms for forensic value and repeatability.

2

Do Bullets Tell Tales?

Validity of Bullet Fingerprinting

Nell Boyce

The ballistics expert left no room for doubt. Testifying November 6 in the trial of accused sniper suspect John Allen Muhammad, he asserted that bullets from victims' bodies matched the rifle found in Muhammad's Chevrolet Caprice "to the exclusion of all other firearms." But the same day, in a Baltimore courtroom, ballistics itself was on trial. There, a federal judge agreed to examine the scientific foundations of bullet matching before deciding whether an expert's assertion of a "match" could be admitted in an upcoming murder trial.

That hearing is just the most recent challenge to bullet "fingerprinting." Forensic science looks little short of miraculous on television shows like CSI, but in the real world, old-time techniques like fingerprint and handwriting analysis have come under fire from critics who say they don't meet the same scientific standards as newer tools like DNA tests. Now, defense lawyers and scientists are leveling the same charge at two mainstays of bullet matching: lead analysis, which links bullets based on chemical traces in the metal, and ballistics, which relies on the distinctive marks that a gun leaves on a bullet. Critics say a bullet lead match can mean little, while claims of a ballistics match often boil down to "I know it when I see it."

Jacqueline Behn, whose brother, Michael, is now in a New Jersey prison, says she's waiting with "bated breath" for a report on lead matching, due out any day now from the National Academy of Sciences. Six years ago, Michael was convicted of murder largely because a box of cartridges he owned had the same chemical fingerprint as bullets found at the murder scene. Experts have testified at hundreds of trials that bullets with matching lead profiles must have been made from the same batch of metal--and thus could have had the same purchaser.

Do Bullets Tell Tales? by Nell Boyce from US News & World Report, November 24, 2003. Reprinted by permission.

But Behn enlisted outside scientists to look at the technique. They found that batches of lead actually aren't necessarily unique, raising the chance of a random match. These days, researchers like statistician Alicia Carriquiry of Iowa State University say that it's "reckless" to give much weight to a lead match. The technique may soon get an official no-confidence vote: One insider says the upcoming NAS report should put an end to "business as usual" for lead matching.

Ballistics evidence like that introduced in the sniper trial-- based on the marks and grooves on bullets and casings--faces a different kind of challenge. Here, the question is: What makes a match?

Bar code. Spent cartridge cases bear impressions from gun parts like the firing pin, and bullets flying down a gun barrel pick up long scratches that look like a bar code. These marks can reveal the gun model, and experts say that the subtlest of them often amount to a "fingerprint" unique to a single gun. When examiners see "sufficient agreement" between cartridges or bullets from the crime scene and ones test-fired from a suspect's gun, they declare a match. For comparison, they also look at "known nonmatches," ammunition fired from other, similar guns.

But what's "sufficient" is often just an examiner's opinion, skeptics say. Deciding which microscopic marks really matter is no mean feat. Nicks and imperfections on gun-making tools can leave the same impressions on multiple guns. The flaws on gun components--and the marks they leave on bullets--can change over time. And proficiency tests show that examiners do make errors; one study of tests from 1978 to 1991 found an error rate of 12 percent. The test-takers almost always erred by saying "inconclusive" instead of the correct answer, and false matches were rare. But examiners know when they're taking a test for a grade. In the real world, they may more readily declare a "match" in a borderline case.

Joan Griffin, a Boston defense attorney with an engineering background, recently questioned the science of ballistics in a retrial of a man previously convicted of shooting at a policeman. The jury acquitted, with one juror later saying the ballistics "match" didn't seem convincing. Other lawyers have followed Griffin's lead. At the hearing in Baltimore, defense attorney Carroll McCabe grilled firearms examiner Karen Lipski about how she had linked two sets of spent casings--one from an incident in which McCabe's client pleaded guilty to firing a gun and the other from a murder scene. In neither case did police recover a gun for firing test bullets.

Lipski said her conclusion was based on "a lot of experience and knowing what you're looking at." She took no photos of the marks and, when asked repeatedly to quantify the correlation needed for a match, replied that McCabe should stop focusing on "the number thing."

Scrambling. That type of testimony is all too common, says Bruce Moran, a firearms examiner with the Sacramento County district attorney's office in California. Now that lawyers have started asking hard questions about the technique's scientific validity, says Moran, "we're all basically caught with our pants down, to tell you the truth. We're all scrambling to address these issues."

Moran sees a place to start. Based on studies of spent bullets from many different guns, firearms experts recently proposed a standard criterion for declaring a match, based on a minimum number of consecutive matching lines left by flaws in the gun barrel. Moran and some other experts are pressing for their colleagues to adopt this universal standard and use it in court, backing up all claims with photographs.

But no such criterion exists for cartridge cases. And even for bullets, experts currently can't determine the chances of a random match--standard practice in forensic DNA analysis. When DNA matching emerged in the 1980s, scientists studied DNA in the general population to quantify the chances of a random match. While often very low, the risk is never zero, so the jury is always told the numerical odds.

Ballistics could someday have that kind of statistical sophistication, says Benjamin Bachrach of Intelligent Automation, who has federal funding to study the uniqueness of the markings guns leave. His company has developed technology that scans a bullet to render a 3-D profile of all the grooves and marks. A computer can then compare bullet scans and calculate the degree of difference. Bachrach says his preliminary work confirms that guns often do create distinctive marks. "The examination of firearms evidence is not a hoax."

Still, "as with everything in life, there's no yes-or-no answer. There's a statistical answer," Bachrach says. When his computer system compares two bullets and comes to a conclusion, "it's not an opinion; it's a number."

Part 5

Blood Evidence

1

Blood Spatter Interpretation at Crime and Accident Scenes

A Basic Approach

Louis L. Akin

Many new technologies can help law enforcement personnel solve crimes and apprehend offenders. While specialists in these fields must keep abreast of new developments, law enforcement personnel do not have to become experts to take advantage of the innovations or to apply the scientific methods. For example, once, albeit a long time ago, authorities often ignored fingerprint evidence at crime scenes because they either did not understand its value or did not have skilled personnel to process it. As specialists became available, however, law enforcement agencies began collecting the evidence. Today, it would prove a misfeasance for an officer or crime scene technician to ignore fingerprints at the scene of a violent crime.

Blood spatter analysis requires the same expert interpretation as fingerprints. Yet, at crime scenes today, authorities often treat blood stains the same as their counterparts did fingerprints a century ago: not routinely measuring or properly photographing them. In many trials, the story composed by the blood that could help law enforcement understand more about what happened during a violent attack or prove a defendant's version of the incident improbable or impossible never gets told.

In the future, resident blood spatter analysts may become as common as fingerprint experts in law enforcement agencies; however, the lack of these specialists in no way should preclude obtaining vital blood spatter evidence at crime scenes. Officers or technicians do not have to interpret the blood spatter but only

Blood Spatter Interpretation at Crime Scenes and Accident Scenes by Louis L. Akin from FBI LAW ENFORCEMENT BULLETIN, March 2005. Reprinted by permission of the author.

measure it, record their findings, and photograph the stain so experts can analyze it later.

EVIDENCE VALUE

Recording blood spatter evidence requires little training. Officers and technicians do not have to learn the trigonometric formulas and calculations involved in interpretation. Measurement training does not require weeks of classroom lectures and months of on-the-job experience. Instead, law enforcement personnel can learn the measurement and photography procedures in 2 days at police academy classes, college criminal justice courses, or in-service seminars.

How much knowledge do officers and crime scene technicians need to preserve blood spatter evidence? First and foremost, they must recognize the importance of the evidence--equal to that of fingerprints, shell casings, bullet holes, or murder weapons. Next, they need to understand that blood spatter indicates the direction from which it came. Then, they must learn how to measure the length and width of a single blood drop, how to tell the direction of travel (visible with the naked eye), and how to find the distance from the drop to the point from which the blood came (also visible with the naked eye). Finally, they need to record those measurements. A form with columns can create a permanent record of the blood spatter evidence at a crime scene. These measurements and the photographs are all an expert requires to analyze the evidence at a later time.

A basic understanding of blood spatter analysis allows the first responding officer, crime scene technician, or detective to assist in correctly collecting and preserving blood stain data at the scene. The principles and procedures are not complicated. The interpretation of blood spatter patterns at crime scenes may reveal critically important information, such as the positions of the victim, assailant, and objects at the scene; the type of weapon used to cause the spatter; the minimum number of blows, shots, or stabs that occurred; and the movement and direction of the victim and assailant after bloodshed began. It also may support or contradict statements given by witnesses. (1) The analyst may use blood spatter interpretation to determine what events occurred; when and in what sequence they occurred; who was or was not present; and what did not occur. (2)

Officers or crime technicians can record the measurements of the stains needed and leave it to the experts to interpret them. However, officers and technicians should have a basic idea of what the blood spatter means, including--

* an understanding of the three classifications of blood spatter velocity and what they indicate;
* how to tell which way a drop was traveling;
* how to measure the length and width of a stain;
* how to measure from the stain to the point of convergence; and
* how to properly photograph blood stains.

VELOCITIES OF BLOOD SPATTER

The velocity of the blood spatter when it strikes a surface is, within certain limitations, a strong and reasonably reliable indicator of the speed of the force that set the blood in motion in the first place. The classification of the velocity (whether high, medium, or low) is that of the initial force causing the blood to move, rather than the speed of the blood itself as it moves, and is measured in feet per second (fps). High velocity blood spatter, for instance, may have come from a gunshot wound inflicted by a bullet moving at 900 fps, whereas medium velocity may have resulted from a spurting artery or a blunt instrument striking the already bloody head or limb of a victim, and low velocity blood may have dripped from a wound or blood-soaked item.

High Velocity

High velocity blood spatter is produced by an external force greater than 100 fps. The stains, sometimes referred to as a mist, tend to be less than 1 millimeter. Usually created by gunshots or explosives, high velocity patterns also may result from industrial machinery or even expired air, such as coughing or sneezing. In any case, the spatter tends to come from tiny drops of blood propelled into the air by an explosive force. High velocity droplets travel the shortest distance because of the resistance of the air against their small mass.

Medium Velocity

An external force of greater than 5 fps but less than 25 fps causes medium blood spatter. The stains generally measure 1 to 3 millimeters. Blunt or sharp trauma, often from knives, hatchets, clubs, fists, and arterial spurts, can produce such stains.

Most medium velocity stains found at crime and accident scenes form patterns created by blood flying from a body to a surface as a result of blunt or sharp trauma or the body colliding with rounded or edged surfaces. It may result from a punch, stabbing, or a series of blows or, in the case of an accident, the body striking surfaces inside or outside a vehicle. Any object that blocks the blood from falling on the surface where it would have landed, including the victim or the attacker's body or a piece of furniture moved to stage the scene, creates a void space in the stain.

Low Velocity

Low velocity blood spatter is created by an external force less than 5 fps (normal gravity) with the stains generally 3 millimeters and larger. It usually results from blood dripping from a person walking or running or from a bloody weapon. Dripping blood often falls at a 90-degree angle and forms a 360-degree circumference stain when it hits a flat surface, depending, of course, on the texture of the surface. Investigators also may find low velocity blood spatter in the trail of an individual who is bleeding with larger pools of blood indicating where the person paused.

THE BLOOD DROP IN FLIGHT

Experiments with blood have shown that a drop of blood tends to form into a sphere, rather than a teardrop, when in flight. Fresh blood is slightly more viscous than water and, like water, tends to hold the spherical shape in flight.

This spherical shape of blood in flight is important for the calculation of the angle of impact of blood spatter when it hits a surface. That angle determines the point from which the blood originated, called the point of origin (PO).

When a drop of blood strikes a flat surface, the diameter of the drop in flight will be the same as the width of the spatter on the surface. The length of the spatter will be longer, depending on the angle at which the drop hit.

POINT OF CONVERGENCE

A fan-shaped blood pattern found on a floor as the result of a gunshot wound to the head can illustrate the point of convergence. When blood disperses in various directions from a wound, the blood drops tend to fan out. As the drops strike the floor, they elongate into oval shapes. An imaginary line drawn lengthwise through the middle of the oval shape will trace back to the area where the blood came from. Lines drawn through several of the blood spatters will cross at the point where the person was standing, called the point of convergence. Somewhere above that point, the blood originated. If the victim was shot in the head, it may be 4 to 6 feet (roughly the height of an average person) above that point.

CONCLUSION

Blood spatter analysis experts can develop important information from the patterns of blood at a crime scene. First-responding officers, crime scene technicians, and detectives can learn to photograph and preserve the measurements of blood spatter evidence at crime and accident scenes, gleaning a great deal of information without becoming experts themselves. If they properly photograph and accurately measure the length and width of the individual blood spatters and the distance from each spatter to the point of convergence, they can provide the expert analysts with data to make the necessary calculations and draw their conclusions. If agencies fail to obtain measurements and photographs, they risk losing critical information forever. Therefore, the collection of blood spatter evidence must be brought into today's world of technological advances and treated as important, but common, crime scene evidence easily preserved by law enforcement personnel who have acquired the necessary skills with a minimum of time and effort.

BLOOD SPATTER EVIDENCE FORM

Law enforcement personnel can use a form to record the distances of the point of convergence (POC) from two reference points, the same ones used to position other objects in the scene. They enter the width and length of the individual drops, as well as the distance to the POC, and then place the numbers of the photographs taken in the last column. They can use either metric or English measurement. In the sample below, for the point of convergence, the distance from reference point 1 equals 156 cm and from reference point 2 equals 350 cm.

ENDNOTES

1. Stuart H. James and William G. Eckert, Interpretation of Bloodstain Evidence at Crime Scenes, 2d ed. (Boca Raton, FL: CRC Press, 1999), 10-11.

2. The list of precisely what information can be learned by the interpretation of blood stain patterns are similar for Tom Bevel and Ross M. Gardner, Bloodstain Evidence at Crime Scenes, 2d ed. (Boca Raton, FL: CRC Press, 2002); Stuart H. James and William G. Eckert, Interpretation of Bloodstain Evidence at Crime Scenes, 2d ed. (Boca Raton, FL: CRC Press, 1999); Edward E. Hueske, Shooting

Incident Investigation/Reconstruction Training Manual, 2002; Louis
L. Akin, Blood Spatter Interpretation at Crime and Accident Scenes:
A Step-By-Step Guide for Medicolegal Investigators, (On Scene
Forensics, 2004); and Paulette T. Sutton, Bloodstain Pattern
Interpretation: Short Course Manual (University of Tennessee at
Memphis, 1998).

Mr. Akin is a licensed professional investigator in Austin, Texas.

2

Luminol: Shedding the Light on 'Hidden' Evidence

Wonders of Chemistry

Stephanie Smith

Detectives nowadays have a number of advanced modern tools to help them in the pursuit and conviction of criminals: DNA-profiling, computer analysis, and machines to clean up the sound on telephone calls and pin-point the origin of the call are just a few. One of the most fascinating tools is luminol, a chemical compound that reveals the presence of blood, often long after the crime has been 'cleaned away'-or apparently so to the naked human eye!

Silent witness
Not a subject for the squeamish, the use of luminol depends on the fact that, when a crime is committed--in particular a violent crime--small traces of evidence always remain. For example, a murderer can dispose of the victim's body and clean up any blood, but without specialised, heavy-duty cleaning agents, tiny particles of blood will stick to most surfaces for many years. Once the visible residues have been removed, no bloodstains will be seen and the crime scene can look 'clean'. But using luminol can reveal an entirely different picture. Luminol can often expose the true horror of a crime, even years after it was committed.

A light-producing chemical reaction
Luminol (5-amino-2, 3-dihydro-l, 4-phthalazinedione, see Box 1), is a simple compound made up of carbon, nitrogen, oxygen and hydrogen. It was originally discovered in the late 1800s. Luminol

Luminol: Shedding the Light on 'Hidden' Evidence: Wonders of Chemistry by Stephanie Smith from CHEMISTRY REVIEW, February 2005.

is a chemiluminescent compound, meaning that it will release light following a chemical reaction (see CHEMISTRY REVIEW, Vol. 5, No. 3, p. 34). If reacted, luminol emits blue-green light with varying intensity. Human blood contains haemoglobin, an iron-containing pigment used to transport oxygen around the body (Figure 1). When luminol is exposed to blood at a crime scene, the bloodstains glow a blue-green colour due to a chemiluminescent reaction involving luminol and the iron in haemoglobin (Figure 2).

Criminal investigators mix the luminol powder with a liquid containing hydrogen peroxide (H_2O_2), a hydroxide (OH^-) and other chemicals, and pour the liquid into a spray bottle. In places where it is suspected that a crime has been committed, investigators turn the lights out and block all the windows to remove any light, spray the area of interest with luminol, and look for a blue-green glow. If the luminol mixture and haemoglobin come into contact, a reaction occurs between the luminol and the hydrogen peroxide. In this reaction (Figure 3), luminol loses nitrogen and hydrogen atoms, and gains oxygen atoms (i.e. it is oxidised), forming a compound called 3-aminophthalate (3-APA). The reaction leaves the 3-APA in an 'excited', or 'triplet', state--the electrons in the compound are boosted to higher electronic orbitals. As these energised electrons fall back to lower energy levels (back to the 'ground' or 'singlet' state), the extra energy is emitted as a photon of light. The iron in the haemoglobin acts as a catalyst for this process, so that the blue-green light is bright enough to see in a dark room.

A clear picture of events

As well as showing the presence of any traces of blood, luminol can provide additional evidence, often offering a clearer picture as to how the crime was committed. The shape, size and intensity of a bloodstain can support a particular sequence of events. For example, a great intensity of luminol light is often found where the murder was actually committed, and bloody 'drag' marks or footprints can show whether the victim was moved or where the murderer walked. The luminol test is sensitive enough to detect 1 part per million (ppm) of blood. In other words, if there is one drop of blood in 999 999 drops of water, luminol will glow. The luminol test will work even if the blood is many years old.

Conclusive evidence?

A luminol glow doesn't always unequivocally indicate the presence of blood. Luminol can also react with a number of other substances, including metals, paints and some plant matter. However, the glow is characteristic, depending on the way luminol reacts with the materials, and an expert can tell the difference. Photographic and video evidence will be recorded at the scene and then further tests can be performed to show conclusively whether or not the substance is human blood.

Another drawback of the luminol test is that it can lead to the destruction of other evidence at the crime scene (including several markers utilised in genetic profiling). For this reason, investigators will usually use luminol only as a last resort, after most other options have been covered.

Despite these disadvantages, the luminol reaction has proved a useful tool for the forensic scientist and the criminal investigator, illuminating evidence that has secured the conviction of several violent criminals. The luminol reaction also has wide application in other fields, including medical science, atmospheric chemistry and analytical chemistry. Luminol is also seen at fairs, concerts and at Hallowe'en, when 'glowsticks' glow with the chemiluminescence of the luminol reaction.

3

The Sins of the Fathers; DNA Fingerprinting

New Developments in DNA Forensics

C riminals in the family? You may now be under scrutiny

Craig Harman was drunk when, in May 2003, he killed Michael Little by throwing a brick from a motorway overpass. He had neither motive nor connection to the victim, meaning that, under normal circumstances, his crime would have been almost impossible to solve. Unfortunately for Mr Harman, he left traces of blood on the brick; even more unluckily, he was related to someone who had once been arrested, and whose DNA was therefore held on a database. On April 19th, he became the first person to be convicted following an investigation into someone else's genetic "fingerprint".

The technique that led police to their man is a novel but straightforward one. Scientists at the Forensic Intelligence Bureau coded the DNA recovered from the crime scene as a 20-number sequence, and fed it into a computer. A few hours later, they had a list of people who shared 11 or more genetic markers with the brick-thrower (while two people chosen at random are likely to share six or seven markers, 11 or more suggests a blood relative.)

Two basic assumptions helped to narrow the list further, according to Jonathan Whitaker, a senior scientist at the bureau. "First, offenders tend to commit crimes on their own doorstep, and, second, family members don't move far away from one another." Having counted out faraway and genetically dissimilar people, investigators were left with a local man whose DNA shared 16 markers with the blood sample. He was Mr Harman's brother.

Britain leads the way in this sort of genetic sleuthing, mostly because the national database is large enough to make "low stringency" searches, which locate partial matches, worthwhile. For years, the police have scraped tissue from the mouths of people charged with offences that carry a prison term, whether or not the case goes to trial. This month, they began taking swabs from people merely arrested for such crimes, with all the resulting genetic fingerprints being held indefinitely. Such zeal explains why, since 1995, the National DNA Database has collected 2.3m genetic profiles, representing 5% of the adult population (and 9% of all men). This is more than any other country in the world: in America, by contrast, the FBI's database holds profiles for less than 1% of adults.

So far, DNA profiling has achieved good results without attracting much controversy. It has made it easier to clear up crimes like domestic burglary, where detection rates stand at 48% when DNA is recovered (compared with 14% when it is not). Tight control over laboratories has allowed Britain to avoid the sort of scandals that have cast doubt on DNA testing in America.

And, until this week, most people reckoned they couldn't be traced through their genetic profile unless they had already had a brush with the law themselves. The technique used in the Harman case changes all that. A method that has, for the past two decades, been used almost entirely to identify or rule out known individuals can now be used to find people through their black-sheep relations.

At [pounds sterling]5,000 ($9,000) a throw, family searches are still too expensive for police forces to request them in any cases other than the most serious. But the technology is likely to become cheaper and more sophisticated, which will produce problems as well as benefits. Since the arrest of one person makes it easier to trace members of their family, and since police investigations produce yet more DNA for the database, there is a danger that the criminal justice system will be seen as picking on a few clans. One solution would be to collect everyone's data, says Chris Asplen, a legal adviser on DNA. "That would be a much more egalitarian system than one where you shop for people's relatives."

4

Modern-Day Fingerprinting

Spitzer's Plan is Right Approach to DNA

Gov. Eliot Spitzer knew where to draw the line in his proposal to expand the state's DNA database. He would require DNA samples from anyone convicted of a crime. "Convicted" is key. Previous proposals that would have required samples from everyone charged with a crime went too far. Forcing people who are presumed innocent to give up their DNA would be an invasion of privacy with troubling potential for misuse. Spitzer's proposal would avoid that pitfall while making better use of DNA technology to catch the guilty, exonerate the innocent and, above all, deliver justice for crime victims. The legislature should get on board.

Currently, only people convicted of felonies and select misdemeanors must submit DNA samples -- about half the defendants convicted of crimes. Spitzer would require samples from all the rest, as well as registered sex offenders and anyone on probation or parole.

State officials would be directed to establish best practices for the collection and preservation of the DNA data. That's important. The state already has a backlog of samples to be tested. Increasing that number won't deliver much in enhanced law enforcement unless the work of collecting and indexing the samples and checking for matches is done quickly and capably. State lab capacity was expanded last year, and testing the surge of new samples could be outsourced, if needed, at an eventual cost of $1.75 million.

Just as important as convicting the guilty is clearing the innocent. Spitzer would allow defendants to demand DNA tests, when appropriate, and prosecutors would be compelled to inform the courts of exculpatory evidence. Also proposed is a state office to study cases of people convicted and later exonerated, to determine how things went wrong.

"Modern-Day Fingerprinting" from NEWSDAY, 2007. Reprinted by permission of Los Angeles Times.

DNA is a powerful tool that should be used but not abused, a balance that Spitzer has gotten just about right.

Part 6

Fingerprinting

1

Northrop Grumman Develops Search Capability for Mobile Electronic Fingerprinting for the U.K. Police Service

Northrop Grumman Corporation (NYSE:NOC) has developed a database search capability for new electronic mobile fingerprinting technology for the U.K.'s Police Information Technology Organisation (PITO) that will help speed up the process of establishing a person's identity. The U.K. police recently launched a pilot program, called the Lantern Project, using this search capability on Nov. 22 in Luton, U.K.

The search capability developed for the electronic mobile fingerprinting devices will enable the U.K. police to capture an individual's fingerprint details in an operational environment for the first time and allow real-time searching of the U.K.'s national fingerprint database on the national identification system, known as IDENT1. The IDENT1 system allows routine identification of suspected criminals throughout the U.K. mainland with a unified collection of finger and palm prints as part of an integrated computer system designed to link more than 50 police forces and agencies in the U.K. Northrop Grumman was awarded the contract to provide PITO with the IDENT1 system in 2004.

"The electronic mobile fingerprinting capability will accelerate the identification process of individuals during roadside stops, therefore decreasing the time police officers spend at their stations, said Hugh Taylor, vice president of Northrop Grumman Information Technology sector. "This process improvement will

.

allow police officers to spend more time on the front line, focusing on their public safety mission and making informed decisions."

The Lantern electronic mobile fingerprinting device sends a scan of both index fingers of the subject to the central fingerprint database using encrypted wireless transmissions. A real-time search against the IDENT1 national fingerprint collection of 6.6 million prints is then conducted. Any possible matches are identified and returned to a police officer in a target time of less than five minutes.

The Lantern pilot project will aid the development of a national U.K solution for use by all police forces by demonstrating how it performs in an operational environment. Ten U.K. police forces are participating in the Lantern pilot project. The pilot is scheduled for completion in December 2007.

Northrop Grumman Corporation is a $30 billion global defense and technology company whose 120,000 employees provide innovative systems, products, and solutions in information and services, electronics, aerospace and shipbuilding to government and commercial customers worldwide.

2

Palm Reading Joins Ranks of the Crime-Fighting Tools

New Fingerprinting Scanners Save Police Time

Tony C. Yang

C at burglars and serial criminals beware: Palm readers have joined the Chicago Police Department. The electronic kind, not the supernatural. In the next two weeks, high-tech scanners that digitally record the entire palm--an upgrade of the department's nine-year-old fingerprinting technology--will be added to every police district, making it more efficient to process arrests. The new Live Scan fingerprint and palm print scanning consoles look like fancy copy machines and will allow police stations access to the main police computers. They will also permit faster and better communications with state and federal authorities, said Marikay Hegarty, director of the record services division. Arrests still require people, added Albany Park District Police Cmdr. Charles Dulay. "You still need good old-fashioned cops and technicians to get [the bad] guys," he said.The paperwork, however, is easier. Previously, the booking process was an ink-stained affair that ate up time as police waited for results from headquarters or the FBI. Now, they are able to find out within minutes if someone in custody has a criminal background. Innocent parties are released faster. It's also easier on police, who have had some form of digital fingerprinting since 1992, but rarely had the time or means to make palm prints mandatory-- even though some 30 percent of crime scene prints are of palm and not fingerprints. The 37 Motorola palm reading units were purchased for $829,000 with a grant from the Illinois Criminal Justice Authority and matching city funds.

Palm reading joins the ranks of the crime-fighting tools: New Fingerprinting scanners save police time by Tony C Yang from CHICAGO TRIBUNE, November 30, 2006. Reprinted by permission of TMS Reprints.

Part 7

The Future in Forensics

1

Deception Detection

Brain Fingerprinting Spots Crime and Innocence

Neil Parmar

Imagine a suspected criminal facing a computer screen while strapped to an electrode-studded headband. Details known only by the police and the perpetrator--crime-scene photos or phrases such as butcher knife--flash on the screen. If a suspect recognizes the stimuli, the brain involuntarily emits an incriminating brain wave.

The scenario's not as far-fetched as it sounds. Indeed, so-called brain fingerprinting has been proved to work in nearly 200 tests conducted in the past 15 years--many by the FBI, CIA and U.S. Navy.

While lie-detector tests measure sweating and heartbeat changes, brain fingerprinting records an electric signal called a MERMER emitted by the brain before the body physically reacts. "It does not test absolute truth or the contents of memory," says Lawrence Farwell, the neuro-scientist who founded Brain Fingerprinting Laboratories in Fairfield, Iowa. Farwell notes the test is voluntary and can only be requested by a suspect if investigators have plenty of specific evidence related to the crime.

Some scientists argue the technology isn't ready for widespread use in the criminal court system. However, an Iowa judge ruled brain fingerprinting admissible in court in 2001 after it was tested and peer-reviewed in the Journal of Forensic Sciences. Last year, the Iowa Supreme Court exonerated a convicted murderer through brain fingerprinting. The man had spent 25 years in prison.

Brain fingerprinting could prove contentious, says Wrye Sententia, director of the Center for Cognitive Liberty and Ethics in Davis, California. She fears the technology could be used to incriminate people, such as suspected terrorists, by bypassing courts. "That's not how our legal system is built," she says. "You're presumed innocent until proven guilty, and this turns the law on its head."

2

'Brain Fingerprinting' Could Change Lie-Detector Tests

Elizabeth G. Book

The Farwell method of brain fingerprinting is a new technology applicable for investigating crimes and exonerating innocent suspects, with a record of 100 percent accuracy in research on FBI agents, U.S. government agencies and field applications, said officials.

Brain fingerprinting determines scientifically whether a suspect has the details of a crime stored in his brain. The system watches for a particular brain response that happens automatically whenever the person sees something familiar.

The technology is ready for implementation by government, military and industrial organizations, in the areas of counter terrorism, counter intelligence, counter espionage, counter-industrial espionage and other crimes, said Nash Thompson, of Brain Fingerprinting Laboratories' international operations department.

"Brain Fingerprinting technology can assist government, military and corporate authorities in the implementation of scientific, external and internal, criminal and non-criminal investigations for various purposes," Thompson said. For example, "this technology can be particularly relevant in the detection and the identification of hostile espionage agents, or moles, who might be obtaining government, military and/or industrial secrets concerning the program management and manufacturing processes of key defense systems," he said.

Brain Fingerprinting Could Change Lie-Detector Tests by Elizabeth G. Book from NATIONAL DEFENSE, April 1, 2003. Reprinted by permission.

InfoMarks: Make Your Mark

What is an InfoMark?

It is a single-click return ticket to any page, any result, or any search from InfoTrac College Edition.

An InfoMark is a stable URL, linked to InfoTrac College Edition articles that you have selected. InfoMarks can be used like any other URL, but they're better because they're stable – they don't change. Using an InfoMark is like performing the search again whenever you follow the link, whether the result is a single article or a list of articles.

How Do InfoMarks Work?

If you can "copy and paste," you can use InfoMarks.

When you see the InfoMark icon on a result page, its URL can be copied and pasted into your electronic document – web page, word processing document, or email. Once InfoMarks are incorporated into a document, the results are persistent (the URLs will not change) and are dynamic.

Even though the saved search is used at different times by different users, an InfoMark always functions like a brand new search. Each time a saved search is executed, it accesses the latest updated information. That means subsequent InfoMark searches might yield additional or more up-to-date information than the original search with less time and effort.

Capabilities

InfoMarks are the perfect technology tool for creating:

- Virtual online readers
- Current awareness topic sites – links to periodical or newspaper sources
- Online/distance learning courses
- Bibliographies, reference lists
- Electronic journals and periodical directories
- Student assignments
- Hot topics

Advantages

- Select from over 15 million articles from more than 5,000 journals and periodicals
- Update article and search lists easily
- Articles are always full-text and include bibliographic information
- All articles can be viewed online, printed, or emailed
- Saves professors and students time
- Anyone with access to InfoTrac College Edition can use it
- No other online library database offers this functionality
- FREE!

How to Use InfoMarks

There are three ways to utilize InfoMarks – in HTML documents, Word documents, and Email.

HTML Document

1. Open a new document in your HTML editor (Netscape Composer or FrontPage Express).
2. Open a new browser window and conduct your search in InfoTrac College Edition.
3. Highlight the URL of the results page or article that you would like to InfoMark.
4. Right-click the URL and click Copy. Now switch back to your HTML document.
5. In your document, type in text that describes the InfoMarked item.
6. Highlight the text and click on Insert, then on Link in the upper bar menu.
7. Click in the link box, then press the "Ctrl" and "V" keys simultaneously and click OK. This will paste the URL in the box.
8. Save your document.

Word Document

1. Open a new Word document.
2. Open a new browser window and conduct your search in InfoTrac College Edition.
3. Check items you want to add to your Marked List.
4. Click on Mark List on the right menu bar.

5. Highlight the URL, right-click on it, and click Copy. Now switch back to your Word document.
6. In your document, type in text that describes the InfoMarked item.
7. Highlight the text. Go to the upper bar menu and click on Insert, then on Hyperlink.
8. Click in the hyperlink box, then press the "Ctrl" and "V" keys simultaneously and click OK. This will paste the URL in the box.
9. Save your document.

Email

1. Open a new email window.
2. Open a new browser window and conduct your search in InfoTrac College Edition.
3. Highlight the URL of the results page or article that you would like to InfoMark.
4. Right-click the URL and click Copy. Now switch back to your email window.
5. In the email window, press the "Ctrl" and "V" keys simultaneously. This will paste the URL into your email.
6. Send the email to the recipient. By clicking on the URL, he or she will be able to view the InfoMark.